ASSASSINATION & TERRORISM

by David C. Rapoport

Donated To
CAMROSE LUTHERAN COLLEGE LIBRARY

By

Canadian Broadcasting Corporation

Copyright © 1971 by David C. Rapoport
All rights reserved

_____ ISBN 0-88794-068-4

Second Impression 1979

HV
6278
: R36
1971 / 46,635

Printed in Canada for
CBC MERCHANDISING
BOX 500, STATION A, TORONTO M5W 1E6
by Hunter Rose Company Limited

PREFACE

The timeliness of the subjects and the highly favorable reaction to the manuscript persuade me now to publish the talks as they were originally heard. A more extensive, systematic, and documented volume is presently being developed for Columbia University Press, but the conclusions, as far as one can tell, will remain essentially unmodified.

During the period of the scheduled broadcasts a tense situation developed in Canada, and it was suggested that I change the title to *The Politics of Fear* and make one additional alteration. Both suggestions were eminently sensible, but I am happy now that the original text can be published and under the title commissioned by the CBC. A few phrases have been altered to promote clarity and one factual error has been eliminated. I have also added one of my earlier essays "Generations in America" (published in Bernard Crick, ed. *Protest and Discontent*), Nachaeyeff's "Revolutionary Catechism", and an extensive bibliography. "Generations in America" was written immediately before I prepared the talks; it discusses some of the same materials and focuses on the "ambivalent society" which I later took to be a precondition of terrorism. References to Nachaeyeff occurred so often in the talks, a copy of his most notorious work seemed pertinent here.

Although there is considerable literature on particular assassination attempts and specific terror campaigns, very little on the general nature and meaning of the two activities exist. For this reason I thought it unprofitable to attempt to distinguish between a potential audience of intelligent laymen and one of professionals

CAMROSE LUTHERAN COLLEGE
LIBRARY

committed to the study. I assumed simply that the reader or listener knew some history and followed current events regularly. Almost anyone can check most of the information cited, for it comes from traditional histories, available political analyses, and good journalistic accounts. Information, of course, is one thing and interpretations are something else, and I hope that both layman and scholar will find that my interpretations contribute to some useful understandings of the subjects.

My principal regret is that the time constraints of radio broadcasting proved more formidable than expected. I developed discussions of assassination plots against minor officials, government-organized assassination conspiracies, and governmental terror, but it proved impossible to use them. As a partial compensation I have included the sources pertinent, in the bibliography. Items published since my own manuscript was completed are also present. A few (i.e., Havens *et al. The Politics of Assassination,* and Dallin, A. and G. Breslauer, *Political Terror in Communist Systems*) contain very useful bibliographies.

One always incurs debts when preparing a manuscript. I incurred many more important ones than is usual, and it is a pleasure to acknowledge them. Various members of CBC performed extraordinary services. Jeffrey Anderson, London, was most important. He invited me to submit a list of possible topics and then chose the present one. Unexpectedly, I had to leave London before he received final authority to produce the talks. More than 6,000 miles away, I had lost some of my enthusiasm when it became necessary to make the actual recording arrangements myself at a university lingering in shell-shocked coma following campus protests over the Cambodia invasion during May, 1970. Without his encouraging letters and telegrams and production assistance, I never would have had the energy or confidence to proceed. I am also grateful to Janet Somerville and Jim Anderson, Toronto, who were sufficiently impressed with the talks to urge that the series be expanded further, and then brought me to Vancouver, B.C., where Bill Terry quickly and expertly produced the final radio version. Lester Sugarman, Toronto, deserves special thanks for his persistence and patience in overcoming significant unforeseeable obstacles.

Students in two seminars discussed the subjects and I have

profited from their remarks, especially those of Stephen English. Three colleagues, Bernard Brodie, Lou Cantori, and Leo Snowiss, made useful suggestions. My interest in assassination was greatly stimulated by Beate Duncan's questions in 1966. My wife Barbara played a critical role. As always she provided excellent editorial help, but more important during the two hectic months in April and May, 1970, when I wrote the manuscript and made the initial tapes myself, she shouldered many of my normal family responsibilities.

Finally I am grateful to Bernard Crick and Pelican Books for allowing me to republish "Generations in America", and to Robert Payne for his translation of Nachaeyeff's "Revolutionary Catechism" which appeared in *Zero*.

David C. Rapoport
London, Sept. 15, 1971

To the Memory of My Parents, Abraham and Dora Rapoport

CONTENTS

This book contains an expanded version of a series of talks first broadcast during November and December, 1970, as part of the series "Politics and Imagination" on *Ideas*, a radio origination of the CBC Department of Information Programs. The programs were organized in London by Jeffrey Anderson, with the assistance of Janet Somerville and James Anderson, Toronto, and were produced in Vancouver by Bill Terry. The executive producer of *Ideas* is Lester C. Sugarman.

DAVID CHARLES RAPOPORT, 42, is a native of Pittsburgh, Pennsylvania, where he received most of his primary and secondary school education. Prior to completing his doctoral dissertation in political theory (*Praetorianism: Government Without Consensus*, Berkeley: 1960) at the University of California, he served in the U.S. Army (1954-56) and was a student of military history, Kings College, London (1957-59). He was a research associate, Institute of War and Peace Studies, Columbia University (1959-62) and a lecturer in political science, Barnard College, Columbia University (1960-61). In 1962 he joined the department of political science, University of California, Los Angeles, where he is now an associate professor whose principal teaching interest is political philosophy. He has been awarded a variety of fellowships and grants including Social Science Research Council (1957, 1964); Ford Foundation (1965, 1966); University of California Humanities Institute (1967); London School of Economics, visiting fellow (1968); American Council of Learned Societies (1971); and is currently the recipient of an award from the National Institute of Mental Health. Most of his other publications concern conspiracy and corruption, and among his essays are contributions to *Political Studies* (1964, 1968); *Political Science Quarterly* (1968); Samuel P. Huntington, *Changing Patterns of Military Politics* (1962); C. J. Friedrich, *Revolution* (1966); R. Pennock and J. C. Chapman, *Obligation* (1970); and H. H. Turney-High, *Primitive War*, 2nd Ed. (1971). Professor Rapoport is married and has two daughters.

Two summers ago *The Times* of London provided a spectacle which tourists could have regarded as a striking testament to proverbial English eccentricities. In a nation excelling all in its respect for law, and in one of the world's leading conservative newspapers, an editorial asked: when should one assassinate the head of state? A flood of letters poured in, for the question had already been topical for several months. In April on *The Third Programme* Professor Bernard Crick argued that some traditional justifications for assassination were relevant to our world still. His conclusion: a tyrant should always be assassinated — the murder would "be a vindication of freedom and reason". Lest listeners misunderstand the immediate implications of his remarks, he repeated several times that English politicians could not be considered proper targets.

Two months after the broadcast, Edward Hyams published a work entitled *Killing, No Murder*, a title which originally appeared on a pamphlet 300 years ago urging someone, it didn't matter whom, to assassinate Cromwell. Since the Reformation, Hyams noted, Englishmen have been too horrified to consider assassination rationally; a fact he deplores, believing that *if* they could be dispassionate about political murder their liberties would be better protected. Hyams wants to identify the Cromwells among us, but English law typically lags behind the requirements of our times and remains rather priggish about such matters. Under the circumstances he feels that in alerting us his duty has been fully discharged.

Hyams believes that assassins should be used to prevent wars and recommends that the UN create an army of assassins to strike down political leaders who threaten hostilities; the deterrent would be more effective and certainly cheaper than a nuclear weapon. Alas, he laments, the wisdom of his recommendations will never be realized; the public is too old-fashioned and recoils at the very idea of assassination.

If the controversy in *The Times* correspondence column is representative, Mr. Hyams owes his countrymen an apology. They want to discuss the subject, and he even has a sympathetic audience. True, no one wants to give the UN assassination powers because Englishmen do not share Mr. Hyams' extraordinary faith in the wisdom of that body, but the majority of letter-writers agree that their government should seriously consider using assassins to prevent war.

The event occasioning the controversy in *The Times* was the revelation of a secret dispatch. In 1938 General Mason MacFarland advised Whitehall that Hitler was determined to have war and that if he were given leave to shoot the Nazi dictator, millions of lives would be saved. Many readers felt that the general offered sound advice, but some must have been shaken when one letter pointed out that he might have missed, and that the subsequent moral outrage in England could have made it impossible to rally effectively for the war which finally came. The *general* repugnance of Whitehall against employing assassins must have seemed more sensible when *The Times* revealed two days later that the same general in 1950 proposed that he be given a Mosquito bomber to eliminate war plotters in the Kremlin!

The general was only the latest in a long line of Englishmen interested in bizarre proposals to reduce military expenditures. Four centuries ago that wise champion of the supremacy of law, Saint Thomas More, in his splendid little work *Utopia*, considered the case for assassination. The Utopians felt that if kings and ministers realized that they, not the common people, would suffer most in war, the world would be more peaceful; and so Utopians regularly advertised that they would pay a high price for the heads of certain enemy statesmen.

The policy worked; St. Thomas More tells us so. Would he have reported Utopian experience differently if he had lived at the *end* of the Reformation instead of near its *beginning?* Assassins were employed in that period partly because they were thought to be inexpensive diplomatic tools. As wars grew more frequent, more intense, and more prolonged, statesmen learned that the cost of employing an assassin went far beyond the price he asked, but men today are beginning again to argue that it does make sense to use assassins as instruments of foreign policy. Have the questioners concluded that the experience of the Reformation is no longer relevant, or have they simply neglected to take it into account? Whatever the reason, no one mentions that horrible bloodbath.

Perhaps the questioners' failure to allude to the Reformation is understandable. As far as I can tell, no essay in any language evaluating the political effects of assassination during that period exists. Indeed, although assassination is one of the most persistent, conspicuous, and intriguing features of organized political life, the subject still remains in the domain of virgin territory — at least for academics. That monument to "relevant" erudition the current *Encyclopedia of the Social Sciences,* for example, does not discuss assassination or its offspring, terrorism. All my searches for a single systematic treatment have been unsuccessful. When we remember how often assassination is a central theme for great artists such as Shakespeare, Dostoyevsky, and Camus, the obliviousness of academics becomes astounding.

The aim of this short series is to provide the public with some rudimentary analysis and information. My first few talks will treat individual assassinations; the last ones will concentrate on terrorism, assassinations contrived to create a fear sufficient to destroy a whole system. Terrorism implies a movement whose objective can only be achieved by repeated assassinations over relatively long periods of time, for fear dissipates when pressure is relaxed or exercised intermittently.

For the balance of our time today I want to discuss the meaning of the term assassination, indicate the history of the phenomenon in Western civilization, and touch upon our three most important justifications for the act.

The word assassin has an Arabic origin. The 12th-century crusaders brought back tales of a strange religious cult calling themselves the Ismaili, and who, incidentally, led by the Aga Khan still survive today. The early Ismaili aimed to purify through

3

terror a corrupt Islam by murdering all its major officials. Ortho-dox Moslims called members of the cult *Hashishaya*, the source of our term assassin. *Hashishaya* also means drug addict and gave rise to our term hashish.

What is the connection between the two terms which appear to have such different connotations? Marco Polo, who studied the Assassins, thought that they were drug addicts. Today we be-lieve that Moslems likened the Ismaili to the drug addict because both attempted to get out of the world of ordinary or common-sense distinctions. It seems probable also that immediately before his foul deed, the Ismaili took drugs to screw up his courage.

To the ordinary Moslem the word *Hashishaya* clearly has a peculiar and specific set of connotations. Many of these repugnant associations are mirrored in our word assassin too. But as we shall see in later talks, our term terrorist more perfectly parallels the Arabic *Hashishaya*, and Moslems themselves do have separate terms to correspond to our assassin and terrorist.

What does the term assassin mean to us? It means murderer but more than that it means an unprovoked murderer who kills in a particularly vile manner. In the common law assassination is murder committed without warning by stealth, surprise, or lying in wait. The assailant has been hired for the occasion, or he under-takes it for political purposes. In any case the victim, usually though not necessarily a prominent person, has not provoked the assault by offering the assassin a personal offense.

So invidious does an assassination appear, that it is a felony to urge one publicly in virtually *all* countries today. Even the English who are notoriously tolerant of free speech, may give one ten years for urging assassination, as a writer in 1881 exulting over the murder of the Russian Tsar, and hoping that he would not be the last killed, learned. To be sure, the laws of all these states betray inconsistencies; if an assassin escapes to a neighboring country, he can claim sanctuary, giving rise to all sorts of potential ironies and problems. Had the assassins of the Russian Tsar reached Eng-land they would have been free men, although an English resident who commended their action might have found himself in jail! Of course assassins do not always claim sanctuary, for fear of identifying themselves to revenge-seekers. Martin Luther King's assassin entered England without revealing his identity, and much to their relief the authorities were able to extradite him.

The laws of the Western world define assassination as a *sneak* attack by a person not personally provoked by his victim. He kills for money or for a political cause. In the formative period of the Western state, the medieval period, an assassin seemed a totally dishonorable or unchivalrous person. The idea of honor, which was derived incidentally from the barbarian and pagan tribes of northern Europe, impelled men to state their hostility publicly, giving their enemy opportunity to withdraw if he chose not to fight. The medieval knight was a ferocious adversary who would kill when provoked, but his honor demanded that the enemy be given a chance to defend himself, and the chivalrous knight could not serve any master who asked him to lay honor aside. The sentiment still had compelling force in the 1930s. When Whitehall rejected MacFarland's offer to assassinate Hitler, it termed the proposal "dishonorable and unsportsmanlike". Thirty years later many of *The Times*' readers found Whitehall's statement "trivial, surprising, and anachronistic". Perhaps it is a telling comment on the mentality of our generation that we find a concern for honor a trivial sentiment. And if the desire to be honorable has become surprising and anachronistic, then it is clear that we are losing our grip on the major historical barrier to the assassination impulse in the West.

Of course, assassinations occurred in the medieval world. Some betrayed their honor and others found serving a cause to be a higher moral ideal. But not until the Reformation, when long tirades against the ideal of chivalry were regularly issued from the pulpits, did assassination become common. Many, however, remained true to the ideal of honor and exercised an incalculable restraining influence on religious passions. Montesquieu states their position most eloquently:

> There is nothing so strongly inculcated in monarchies by honor as submission to the prince's will; but this very honor tells us that the prince ought never to command a dishonorable action, because that would render us incapable of serving him. Crillon refused to assassinate the Duke of Guise, but offered to fight him instead. After the Massacre of Saint

> Bartholomew, Charles IX sent orders . . . for the
> Huguenots to be murdered. Viscount Dorté, who com-
> manded at Bayonne, wrote to the King, 'Sire, among
> the inhabitants of this town and Your Majesty's troops,
> I could not find so much as one assassin; they are
> honest citizens and brave soldiers. We jointly, there-
> fore, beseech Your Majesty to command our arms and
> lives in things that are practicable!' This great and
> generous soul looked upon a base action as a thing
> impossible. There is nothing that honor more strongly
> recommended to the nobility than to serve their prince
> in a military capacity because its successes and even
> its miscarriages are the road to grandeur. Yet this very
> law of its own making, honor chooses to explain, and
> in case of any affront it requires or permits us to retire.

After the Reformation the ideal of honor gained new strength. Eighteenth-century man felt that *how* one played the political game was more important than whether one won or lost, and it is not surprising to find that age virtually immune to assassination plots.

The French Revolution and the Romantic Movement harnessed passions once again to the success of abstract causes. Winning the game became all important. Although governments still retained profound contempt for employing assassins, citizens began striking down public figures with frightening regularity. The great period occurred between 1865 and 1914, beginning with the murder of Lincoln and ending with that of Archduke Franz Ferdinand. One head of state or major minister fell nearly every eighteen months. Reacting to this wave of senseless assassinations, *The Spectator* commented that unless Europeans refused to justify *all* assassinations whatsoever, there would be no end to the turn-of-the-century madness. And in a subsequent editorial seven years before the event *The Spectator* prophesied that some fanatic would probably kill an Austrian prince and trigger the greatest war in history.

After the Great War ended, assassination became less common in most countries, but during the past decade the movement has been in the other direction. We still have much ground to cover before we can match the record set in the 19th century, principally by the Anarchists. But it still may be done. The revival of Anarchist influence in recent years has produced only a few assassinations so far, but it may be only a matter of time before the incitements to violence in the literature of the New Left have their full effects.

If the sole animating force in Western civilization had been the notion of honor, assassinations would be virtually "unthinkable" or at least we would be unable to supply an acceptable public justification. But our approaches to moral questions are shaped by a variety of other seminal sources as well, and we have developed three major justifications for assassination. One can conceive it in purely instrumental terms — the moral value depending entirely on the end achieved, a typical Greek and Roman view. One can admit that assassination is evil, but nonetheless justifiable occasionally to prevent a greater evil, a Christian approach. Finally, some believe that assassination is always good in itself regardless of the end achieved, a modern terrorist position. For the remainder of this talk I shall focus on the first two views, the Greco-Roman and the Christian.

The ancient Greeks and Romans had no word to correspond to our term assassination. A killing was simply a means to an end; its moral significance depended entirely on the *nature* of the person killed. A man who struck a public personality down was either a murderer or a tyrannicide. And the word for tyrannicide was the same as that for "liberator", one who freed his country.

Cicero's discussion of tyrannicide represents the conventional attitude. A tyrant, or one who aims at tyranny, was a public enemy; every citizen was *obliged* to kill him as quickly and efficiently as possible. Cicero produces no ethical or political arguments to justify treachery or the abandonment of legal procedure; his audience understands that the tyrant is one who means to subvert all conventions himself, and that it would be foolish to bind oneself by rules which the tyrant means to destroy. The idea that the method of killing tyrants involved moral questions would have been as preposterous as the notion that it might be morally wrong to put out fire with water, or to shoot a wild beast from behind.

Perhaps the more peculiar aspect of the Classical attitude toward *tyrannicide* was that no distinction was made between killing a tyrant and a man who purportedly *aimed* at becoming one. Greek cities, for example, employed town criers to offer rewards for anyone who killed a citizen who was *intending* to become a tyrant. The first three Romans assassinated were *accused* only of aiming at tyranny. Thus, Maelius was a wealthy Patrician holding a minor office who sold corn at very low prices to the plebians during difficult times. Although he did not break any law, the action led Servilius to strike him down, supposedly because he was currying favor with the lower classes. Manlius, a great military leader, angered when one of his most valiant veterans was taken to prison as a debtor, paid the debt, angrily declaring that as long as he, Manlius, possessed a foot of land such inequities would never occur again. The speech provoked an assassin's knife. Spurius Cassius was the author of a land reform bill which struck some as a step to tyranny, whereupon his own father assassinated him. In the earliest accounts the assassins did not submit their actions to judicial inquiry. The tyrant or would-be tyrant simply had no rights in law. Later, assassins are compelled to justify their deeds, but since the victim could hardly respond to accusations, a fair trial was impossible. Small wonder that our greatest student and admirer of Rome, Theodor Mommsen, throws up his hands in disgust!

Xenophon says that the tyrant-killer was never punished, and that a grateful people usually placed statues in temples to commemorate his deed. Cicero notes that the Roman regarded tyrannicide as "the finest of all glorious deeds, *especially* if the tyrant had previously been an intimate friend". Some of the most celebrated figures in Greek and Roman history were tyrant-killers. Brutus, who murdered Caesar, his friend and benefactor, was a member of a family which contained several generations of tyrant-killers.

One should emphasize that the willingness to sanction *any* means to rid the state of a potential tyrant had different implications in various stages of Roman history. When the citizen body was small and everyone knew everyone else, tyrannicide was extremely rare. Later, during the Empire, when Roman territories comprehended some three million square miles, the story was very different. The surviving rhetoric texts tell us that the subject became an obsession with academics. Students were compelled to defend their views on hypothetical questions concerning potential tyrants. X does Y, the schoolboy would be instructed. Is he truly a tyrant? If so, how should he be killed? What shall be the assassin's reward? The classroom, Tacitus acidly notes, was an arena where troops of students murdered tyrants with volleys of styluses! The Emperors were deeply disturbed with the "busy work" of Roman students; but even though nearly two-thirds were assassinated, none could destroy this perverse educational tradition. Should we be surprised that the Emperors so often seemed paranoid?

Greek and Roman history inspired many generations of students long after the ancient states themselves disappeared. During the Reformation, Hobbes contended that the universities, by celebrating certain Classical texts, bore responsibility for the revival of assassination. When the Duke of Buckingham in 1628 was told he was being stalked by assassins, he responded that although the books of the ancients were cherished as never before, "there are no Romans left". Several days later his widow learned how strong the influence of Rome still was.

In the literature of the French Revolution and that of the Romantic Movement, the invocation to Brutus and a whole host of legendary Classical heroes appears over and over again. When Charlotte Corday goes to Paris to murder Marat, she carries a copy of Plutarch to fortify her determination, and as she is taken to the guillotine the crowd murmurs, "She is greater than Brutus." The German Marxist leader August Bebel, shaken by the massive hatred for the left inspired by the assassinations during the late 19th century, attempted to shift the responsibility to the bourgeoisie by correctly noting that a major cause was the university's inclination to glorify Greek and Roman tyrannicide.

Compared to the Greeks and Romans, early Christians move in an entirely different realm of discourse. Christians do have discussions, open and stated disagreements. Most Christians think tyrannicide always wrong, and none justifies the assassination of one merely *suspected* of aiming at tyranny. Every Greek or Roman would reject both propositions.

St. Thomas Aquinas offers a typical Christian justification. Assassination is evil but in special circumstances permissible: those circumstances are (1) that the victim has actually usurped power by violence; (2) that he has violated moral law; (3) that he remains a persistent threat to the lives and morality of his subjects; (4) that one can be reasonably certain that the murder will produce a better state of affairs; and finally, (5) that no other remedy is available. For the Christian, as opposed to the Greek, assassination is a *right* but never a *duty*, and everyone who claims that right is obliged to submit himself to judicial inquiry afterwards.

Even St. Thomas More, though less restrained than most Christian writers, limits the right of assassination carefully. Governments alone are permitted to plot assassinations and only to prevent war or to reduce its scale. Foreigners are hired to do the dirty job, men who are inclined to do anything for money anyways. More even prohibits assassins who have murdered on Utopia's behalf from seeking refuge on the island, lest they contaminate virtuous citizens!

To the great body of Christians, therefore, the attitude towards assassins is mixed or ambivalent. Christians have always been apprehensive of the possibility that in regarding assassins as heroes, they might be opening a Pandora's box. Dante, the last medieval Christian thinker, places Brutus in Hell; whereas the ancients certainly would have put him in Heaven if they had been aware of its location.

The Christian approach to assassination still dominates us today. Occasionally, we might think it permissible to assassinate, but the assassin himself even in these situations thinks that he will be punished if caught and we rarely admire him. How many assassins, for example, can you think of who are celebrated as heroes? The English do commemorate a would-be assassin, Guy Fawkes, but it is his failure, not his victory, which they celebrate. One striking example of an assassin still remembered as a glorious figure exists — the legendary William Tell. There are a few others though far less famous; virtually all, like Tell, tried to free their people from foreign oppression. It is worth stressing, to indicate the remarkable continuity of our tradition, that the celebrated assassins of the Bible, Ehud, Jehu, and Judith, persons whose deeds are frequently cited by Christian writers, also struggled to keep their people from submitting to a foreign yoke. Nonetheless, the number of honored assassins even in this category is very small.

Attitudes towards assassination are related to a people's understanding of the status of their enemies. The Greeks and Romans felt that an enemy had no rights: inventing the idea of total war, they practised assassination as one aspect of it. A Christian knight like Galahad or Roland worried about the difference between fair and foul fighting; to an Achilles or a Ulysses the distinction would be incomprehensible. The Greek or Roman went to war like a wild creature uncaged, massacring entire populations, or selling them into slavery if that were more expedient. Whatever he did, he never felt required to justify himself; the enemy had no rights and *every* member of a hostile population was in the same category. The Christian was more discriminating; not everything was permitted, even in a war of defense — the only kind a Christian could in good conscience undertake. The quarrel was between states, not populations, and the soldier who surrendered should not be killed. The Christian always distinguished between soldiers and civilians, male and female, adult and child.

Some might argue that such elaborations are foolish, for once war begins expediency alone should be our guide. But the Christian feels that not all rights are suspended simply because a war is in process. Christians do not always practise what they preach; moreover, in the Reformation many Christians began preaching different doctrines and wars began to be understood in Greek or Roman terms. Still, the ensuing bloodbath made Christians recoil, and in the 17th century the idea of limited war revived again. Since the French Revolution we have again become more receptive to the idea of total war, though we still draw lines at assassination and at a number of other critical points. Moreover, the Christian ideal seems to have great influence and, paradoxically, often thrives among those who openly proclaim themselves to be non-believers. Is it only the Christian believer who is disturbed by the facts that the American involvement in Vietnam is difficult to justify as a war of defense, that the distinction between soldier and civilian is often violated, and that allegations concerning massacres and tortures are frequently made?

So much for our introductory remarks on justification. Next time we shall elaborate a few related issues and move on to a more concrete discussion of assassination plots.

POLITICAL AND TACTICAL
INFLUENCES ON ASSASSINATION

Last time I discussed justifications for assassinations. Today I will discuss circumstances shaping assassination plots. First, three political considerations will be treated: the role of justification, the importance of groups which find their unity in a common creed, and the significance of personality. Subsequently, I will take up tactical dimensions or those problems which all assassins must overcome to get within striking range of their victims.

You will recall the distinction between Greco-Roman and Christian justifications. The ancients always visualized assassination in instrumental terms, moral value being determined *solely* by the results produced. Christians understood the act as evil but sometimes justifiable to prevent a greater evil. Obviously, a distinction between an assassin's real motive and his public justification may exist. Nonetheless, if he wants others to applaud the deed or find it inspiring, he must use the language of justice and appeal to aspirations and conditions which everyone can understand and share. It follows that the mode of justification possible shapes the assassin's problems and conduct in gross and subtle ways. Jealousy may have driven Cassius to plot Caesar's death, as Shakespeare suggests, but Shakespeare knows that there would be no chance for the conspirators to escape if Brutus, whose motives were unimpeachable, refused to participate. Hypocrisy, indeed, is the tribute vice must always pay to virtue.

The general attitudes of the whole body politic towards assassination deter or incite plots; they may even influence the assassin's social origin! Every Greek or Roman child was inspired by glorious stories of tyrannicide. Those best inculcated with the national tradition, the *better* men (who in the normal course of events had held or would hold high public office) furnished the largest number of assassins.

Because Christians could not honor assassins, the incentive to become one was reduced and assassins came increasingly from the lesser classes. Ambitious notables might still plot, but it was dangerous and unnecessary to reveal their role. Christians, therefore, often hired assasins — the Renaissance even had a special name for hired assassins, *bravi*. This was only one of the many ways in which the necessity to conceal the plotter's identity was demonstrated. Contrast this pressure with the very different one in the ancient city-state. Only in risking maximum personal danger could a tyrant-killer receive the full acclaim sought, and so generally the plotter and assailant were the same person.

The dramatic literature of the ancients never visualizes the problem of a concealed assassination, a commonplace theme of our own — witness *Hamlet, Macbeth,* and *Boris Godunov.* Consider Macbeth for a moment; if known as Duncan's assassin he will not survive himself. The deed must be attributed to others. But people wonder why two porters, even in a drunken stupor, should murder their king.

Macbeth did assassinate Duncan. But even if the two porters had done so, the fact that he, not they, gained from the action would always generate potentially disastrous rumors which might never be put to rest. Eight centuries after Becket was cut down in Canterbury Cathedral, historians still debate whether or not the king was involved.

We are all familiar with the Warren Commission's credibility gap. Most Americans still believe that some left- or right-wing organization was responsible. Each time an American President has been assassinated similar rumors have besieged the country, and in the cases of Lincoln, Kennedy, and especially Garfield, citizens have openly suggested that *even* the Vice-President might be implicated.

Psychiatrists attribute the extraordinary spate of rumors to the public's irrationality. There may be a grain of truth in the view, but on the whole — like most psychiatric explanations of political behavior — this one is far too facile. We do not honor assassins, so we find it difficult to understand why a man might become one. On the other hand, it is obvious that *someone* gains when a leader falls. If the assailant himself is cut down before a court has opportunity to examine him, as so often happens, the mystery deepens. Rumors flourish naturally in such situations, and if the public persists in refusing to accept the most reasonable explanation, the difficulty may lie partly with those who offer it. Scepticism about the Warren Commission Report became especially profound after the Vietnam War had seriously undermined the "credibility" of the U.S. government.

A climate which nourishes assassination must be distinguished from one which stimulates violence everywhere. Prior to the collapse of the Republic, Rome, for example, probably experienced *less* internal violence than any other known historical entity. For seven centuries she did not require a police force and permitted no one to carry arms in the city! For two centuries she did not have a death penalty and enjoined magistrates to permit convicts to escape before imprisonment!

The Roman Republic combined an extraordinary respect for law with a striking tolerance for a certain type of assassin. But a community which cannot respect its own law will breed murder everywhere, including all sorts of assassination. The Renaissance city-state is the best case in point. New governments daily came to power by force, to be sustained precariously by police establishments whose numbers and expense stagger the imagination still. "No man," Burckhardt says, "believed any longer in the justice of the law. When a murder was committed, the sympathies of the people ranged . . . instinctively on the side of the murderer." Another prominent historian notes that "each province, each city, each village, became the theater of private feuds and assassinations. Every household was the scene of homicide and empoisonment." In fifty years eleven members of the Medici family, the most prominent in Florence, were murdered, and five others probably died by foul means. The legend was that every Medici believed that he must die by fraternal or paternal hands, and seven of the authenticated murders were committed by members of the family.

Every political community may provide a unique set of justifications to would-be assassins. But the internal dynamics of some bodies-politic is animated by separate groups espousing creeds and doctrines, and these may constitute a second, though obviously derivative, influence on assassination patterns. I shall discuss this matter more thoroughly when the terrorist question is explored, but right now it is worth pointing out that in the West, ever since the Reformation began, most assassinations have in some way been related to the existence of doctrinal sects whose ends some members feel are so important that all means, including assassination, seem justified.

Ironically, the victims of doctrinal politics are often cut down by their own followers or rivals. Malcolm X and George Rockwell were assassinated by former associates. Dominant figures in the Irish fight for independence were killed by former followers. The difficulties of Marxist parties are notorious; who can forget Trotsky's fate? Marat was accused of betraying the French Revolution. During the Reformation moderate leaders murdered enthusiasts of the same party and were in turn often the victims of swift retaliation.

When unity depends upon consciously held doctrine, conflicts, even conflicts over tactics, often seem attempts to adulterate or destroy the doctrine, and those conflicts provide the context for accusations of heresy or treason. In all groups heretics or traitors draw more hatred than any other conceivable enemy.

Ceteribus paribus, all things being equal, a politics which creates larger and more visible personalities simultaneously incites and intensifies impulses to assassinate them. A third influence on plot patterns, therefore, is the political importance of the victim. "Why do they want to kill you?" someone asked Malcolm X. "Why can't you see it's because I'm me." Malcolm X was irreplaceable. When he was slain, all threats to Elijah Muhammad's dominance ceased. When Trujillo fell, a revolution ensued in the Dominican Republic. The ancient tyrant, too, dominated solely by virtue of his personality, one reason why patriots felt that he could not remain alive. The tyrant occupied no special office for successors to possess; when a tyrannicide occurred, those who had been in effect paper functionaries while he was alive simply began exercising their offices in the traditional constitutional manner again.

In contrast to these instances a personality may be important because he possesses an office overshadowing all others in the system. Witness the Presidency of the U.S. — an awesome office, whose occupants and candidates have been killed or assailed eight times in the last century.

The predicament of the U.S. is often explained by glib references to her "original sin" — frontier violence. But no U.S. officeholder of any rank was assassinated until 1865, and if insurance policies were written for all office-holders in the contemporary world, the innumerable local, state, and federal officials in the U.S. — with one exception — would be better risks than most of their counterparts abroad. The president or presidential candidates alone constitute a special class.

The president today resembles the 18th-century monarch in being the ceremonial head, the commander-in-chief, and chief executive. Like a modern prime minister he leads the dominant party, but unlike the prime minister he cannot be removed the moment he has lost the confidence of his party. He is the "tribune of the people"; no one else is elected by them all.

Initially, the powers of the presidency were unrealized. Jackson was the first called to be the "tribune of the people", and he also became a target for the first assassin's bullet. Lincoln, the first killed, expanded the powers of the office enormously and is generally regarded as the first modern president. As new powers are added they seem to form an ever-widening series of concentric circles with the president in the center as a bull's-eye. Whatever the most appropriate image, the system does generate intense circuits of affection and hate through one vulnerable point.

Collegial and parliamentary governments change the character of the personal involvements and diffuse tension, so it is not surprising to discover that dividing ceremonial and political functions profoundly affects assassins too. In Europe and the senior Commonwealth states the ceremonial head has been attacked at least as often as the political leader. Only the Russian Tsar, whose powers were truly extraordinary, attracted as many assassins as the American president has.

History demonstrates a relationship between assassination attempts and the degree to which power seems to be held by one man. Among primitives assassination is virtually unknown because power is so remarkably diffused; proverbially the most dangerous and insecure office is always that of the despot in the great Oriental empires. As an extra-constitutional act, assassination necessarily implies the forms it violates.

Just as the political situation influences plot possibilities enormously, so every assassin must calculate how to overcome a set of physical barriers which prevent his access to the intended victim. These barriers shape the assassin's tactical problems and hence the plot patterns in a variety of ways. A hired assassin, for example, may kill loosely guarded persons, such as a party leader or a trade union official, but he rarely attacks a well-guarded one. The reason is obvious: he is unlikely to get away, and one who kills for money aims to enjoy it afterwards. The major exception would be the hired assassin who is part of a larger force which seeks to usurp the powers of government and hence will be in a position to claim immunity — a problem I will discuss next time.

Those who have read Jack London's novel, *The Assassination Bureau Ltd.*, will remember his interesting discussion of the murders one can and cannot buy. The Director of the Bureau explains to a disappointed Anarchist the reason for the great differences in his prices. The Anarchist can afford to buy an assassin for a police chief, but to hire one for a head of state is way beyond his financial means. Even police chiefs are expensive, the Director explains, because the Anarchist needs a spectacular death in a public place to maximize publicity. To save money it is better to buy a poisoner or one who can "arrange an accident", reducing the assassin's personal risks.

If the intended victim is constantly guarded by police and/or friendly crowds, success is related to the value the assassin attaches to his own life. If he is *really* prepared to exchange his life for that of his victim, then, as John Kennedy remarked, days before that fateful moment in Dallas, no one can stop him. Aristotle and Machiavelli agreed.

Machiavelli added that of those determined to sacrifice their own lives, the lone assassin should be feared most. Does his view seem reasonable? A tough old soldier like Caesar might have been a match for a single assassin. The material in Teddy Roosevelt's breast pocket saved him from one assassin's gun; could it have saved him from two? Yes, the objection is obvious, but the lone

assassin always finds it easier to get into striking position unde-
tected, and that is the most difficult problem of all.

There are two phases in every assassination plot: preparation
and execution. In each phase, conspirators necessarily face risks of
detection which the lone assassin can avoid. Most conspiracies fail
in the preparation phase when plans are still being formulated. The
possibilities of being detected are multiplied by the numbers involved and the time necessary to perfect plans. Machiavelli
explains:

> . . . treachery is so common that you can safely impart
> your project only to your most trusted friends willing
> to risk their lives for your sake, or malcontents equally
> desirous of the prince's ruin. Of such reliable friends
> it becomes impossible to find many, for their devotion
> to you must be greater than their sense of danger
> and fear of punishment. Moreover, men are apt to
> deceive themselves as to the degree of attachment
> and devotion which others have for them and there
> are no means of ascertaining this except by actual
> experience. But experience in such matters is of the
> utmost danger [and] . . . if you wish to measure a
> man's good faith by the discontent he manifests, you
> will be easily deceived for by the very act of com-
> municating to him your designs, you give him the
> means of putting an end to his discontent.

Between the reign of Elizabeth and that of William and Mary
there were thirty or forty English plots to assassinate the sovereign.
All failed, the overwhelming majority in the preparation stage, and
mostly because of informers. Even religious fanatics could not overcome this problem. Englishmen will also remember that informers
foiled the last great English plot in 1820, the Cato Street Conspiracy. A more recent example occurred this year in California
when the plot to murder Judge Gittelsohn, who had ruled that
"bussing" children was necessary to ensure "racial balance" in the
schools, was frustrated.

In the preparation phase, conspiracies are frequently revealed
through the carelessness of one participant. Nero was saved when
a conspirator first made his last testament — a deed which made
acquaintances wonder why. Casual remarks would have frustrated

the plot in the film Z had authorities themselves not been involved. Some assassins betray plots because they cannot control their own emotions. People *noticed* that Brutus could not sleep. The housekeeper for General Beck, one of the conspirators in the July plot against Hitler, told the Gestapo that for several weeks before the attempt, the General's sheets had been wet with sweat each morning. On the Ides of March one conspirator was seen talking to Caesar and the others panicked, almost alerting him. Men with guilty consciences always think that everyone else is talking about them.

Compare the conspirators' immense difficulties during the preparation period with the advantages of the lone assassin. He possesses his own secret which he will not consciously betray. The plot may be revealed inadvertently, but even so he need only worry about one man. The critical facts are that very few lone assassins are apprehended before reaching the scene of the crime while most conspiracies fail long before that point.

The problems associated with the execution phase also suggest that conspirators are more likely to be detected before they actually deliver the final death-blow. The longer the time between preparation and execution the more their dangers multiply. If an unforeseen event occurs they face a cruel predicament. In delaying the attack they increase chances for discovery; but in pressing ahead they must act in a more unfavorable context. Time and time again, Machiavelli shows, conspirators have been defeated by this dilemma. A more contemporary illustration is the July Plot against Hitler. When the ventilation in the steel bunker broke down, the meeting convened in a wooden building. In a steel bunker the time bomb's blast would have been contained and all the occupants killed; but the wooden building crumbled, dissipating the force of the explosion in open air. Von Stauffenberg could have postponed the effort, as he had several times before, but months would elapse before another opportunity would occur and the Gestapo had already begun to pick up the trail and would probably have crushed the conspiracy in a week or two.

Assassination teams function as a unit. The constraints on time are so great that the failure of one man to complete his assigned role at the appropriate moment dooms the plot. There are countless examples to illustrate the point. The most notorious of the Renaissance was the Pazzi Plot against Lorenzo de' Medici. An unexpected itinerary change made conspirators decide to kill in the Cathedral. When one refused to murder in a sacred place, the roles were redistributed, leading to serious mistakes. A more recent example occurred in an Irish attempt on Field-Marshal Sir John French. The plotters planned to place a rented cart in the road to stop French's convoy and make it vulnerable to a sneak attack. Unexpectedly the cart proved clumsy, and as they struggled to get it into position, a constable appeared telling them to let the convoy pass first. One conspirator panicked, throwing a grenade at the constable, thus saving the Field-Marshal's life.

Time is the conspirators' most precious and scarce commodity. But the intelligent lone assassin has plenty of time. If circumstances prove inappropriate, he can wait for a better moment—one reason why he is always so dangerous. In deferring action the lone assassin runs the risk of unleashing uncontrollable anxieties in his own soul. In countries where assassination is repugnant, his sense of guilt may be aroused, and everywhere the prospect of his own death may become more and more frightening. Most lone assassins probably abandon their efforts altogether after withdrawing from one attempt. But should one decide to go on, strange things may happen. Like Raskolnikov, the hero of Dostoyevsky's *Crime and Punishment*, a lone assassin may be so overcome by remorse that he feels compelled to confess and/or commit suicide afterwards. James Felton, who struck the infamous Duke of Buckingham down and was the only English assassin who was a public hero for a short time, gave himself up, begging that the hand that did the deed be severed from his body. In Sweden and Finland during the 20th century, two of the four lone assassins committed suicide.

Whether the particular assassin murders *because* he is mad or whether fear or guilt unbalance him *after* he decides to kill, it is striking how often lone assassins appear insane. The M'Naghten rule, the common standard now for testing insanity in English-speaking countries, was developed as the result of an assassination case, an attempt on the Prime Minister Sir Robert Peel. Since then many lone assassins, but *no conspirators*, have been held insane. I have not been able to discover how widely honored insanity pleas are in the contemporary world, but it is worth noting that the officer who fired at Soviet leaders during the January, 1969 Cosmonaut parade is now in a mental institution.

When we remember how powerful the desire for revenge must be when a popular leader is struck down, it is a striking testament to the independence of our courts that they will honor insanity pleas. Cynics will quickly rejoin that the plea is more often accepted when the assassin fails. The more important fact is that courts often spurn public demands for vengeance. South Africa has never, for example, been notoriously tolerant of political deviants; yet when Premier Verwoerd was stabbed to death, the court committed the assailant, insisting that it would be plain murder to do otherwise.

It should be emphasized that the personal histories of lone assassins suggest only that a sizeable *minority* show traces of insanity and that the phenomenon of the crazed assassin came into the Western world after the development of Christianity. The assassin in the Greek and Roman Republics seems in all respects a balanced and competent person both before and after the fatal event. Let the listener interpret these facts as he wishes!

The lone assassin has extraordinary facilities for completing his mission. Why, then, should he seek help or enter a conspiracy? There are many good reasons why he might want assistance: (1) he may want his victim dead soon, (2) he may wish to escape himself and want, as Von Stauffenberg did, to influence subsequent political events, and (3) he may believe that the act is fruitless if others are not assassinated, too.

The lone assassin cannot control the political effects of his action: can his act, then, ever be considered rational? It can in two circumstances; when the political cause he finds so evil depends upon one person and the murder is unlikely to make the situation worse. Alternatively, it may be rational when solid grounds exist for thinking that his act will release beneficial but still dormant forces. We have spoken of the first circumstance already; the last may be illustrated by the socialist leader Friedrich Adler's murder of the Austrian Premier in 1916. Adler hoped to liberate hostility to Austria's continued participation in the war. In court he said:

> I did not think for a single moment of unloosing mass action at this time, but I wanted to create the psychological conditions for future mass action. I did not

> want to make revolution by my deed but I wanted
> to obtain the possibility of revolution — my act was a
> symbolic deed; it would show that one is obliged to
> risk his life for his conviction.

Subsequent events showed that Adler's deed did have profound consequences. It helped the forces opposed to the war, but it also stimulated waves of fanatics who plagued Austrian politics afterwords, setting the stage for the Fascist triumph.

The lone assassin can set furious political forces in motion, but only conspirators have a reasonable chance of controlling them, and the best way to exploit the opportunity provided by an assassination is to usurp the powers of government — the primary subject of our talk next time.

Last time I suggested that assassination always involves important technical problems, the chief one being how to gain access to the victim. No official is ever wholly immune from assassins, for none can isolate himself completely. But insofar as assassins intend a more favorable political situation, they simply cannot be satisfied with murder itself, for they may discover that their deed has made their victim a martyr and destroyed their own cause.

Lone assassins cannot control reactions. Conspirators may be able to do so, but they often fail to make appropriate plans. Some, like Brutus and Cassius, are so certain of a favorable reception that they do nothing to secure it. Others have better reason to avoid making plans for the political aftermath; they know themselves to be too weak to implement them. Note the conspirators who assassinated Lincoln and those who tried to murder Truman.

To maximize possibilities for political success one should seek to control the public's reaction, and obviously the most strategic lever for that purpose is government. In my talk today I will discuss assassination as an aspect of a conspiracy to usurp governmental powers.

Assassination need not be an integral part of a usurpation plot. To understand the relevant considerations a few notes on the character of the usurpation process itself is essential. Successful usurpations involve two steps: the destruction of an existing gov-

*Several critical points in this lecture were suggested by a UCLA undergraduate student, Stephen English.

ernment, and the creation of a new one which includes the usurpers. A government may be overthrown if the public will not rally to its defense, but without appropriate ruling credentials those responsible for the government's destruction will not be recognized as its successor. Often would-be usurpers find that they have only eliminated a government to provide a priceless opportunity for others with better claims to rule. Kurdish officers in Iraq today might be able to topple an existing regime, but the hostility to Kurds is such that they might well be preparing the way for a government which will oppress Kurds even more.

At the moment of their blow, especially if a coup d'état is attempted, the usurpers' forces are greatly outnumbered and cannot afford to stimulate the will to resist before they establish firm control of the administrative apparatus. Hence the manner of the deposition could reveal crucial evidence about the character and intentions of the usurpers, convincing the potential opposition that they must close ranks immediately. In some instances it is even necessary to conceal information about the political identity of the usurpers for a brief but critical moment between the deposition of the old and the establishment of the new government. This is why in Latin America lower-ranked officers, majors, and colonels, prove such excellent conspirators; they have established some administrative credentials, but they are not conspicuous enough for anyone *yet* to have reasons to be against them. When usurpations are common, politics becomes predominantly *negative* in character. In Latin America *no* is easier to say than *yes*, and the future generally belongs to those with the fewest no's registered against them.

Assassination seems a quick and efficient way to remove the most obvious resisters. Undeniably, sometimes this argument is true. Yet when we remember how precarious the initial hold of the usurpers usually is, there must be many circumstances in which caution is advisable. A people may tire of a government but still deplore the assassination of its major personalities. By the time Sukarno was deposed few Indonesians wanted him as their president, but he was after all the "father of his country" and many would have responded to his assassination violently.

No matter how disordered a body politic is, "unnecessary killings" can provoke serious reactions. During the most violent days of the Renaissance in Bologna and Milan, several usurpation attempts failed because assassins enraged the public. In 19th-century Spain uprisings occurred every year or two; nonetheless a government whose police killed more than four rioters in Madrid was generally condemned as being too brutal and forced to resign. When governments have that little credit, usurpers may "manufacture incidents" to impale them. In 1943 unscrupulous Bolivian officers substituted live ammunition for the usual blank cartridges in the rifles of unsuspecting soldiers sent to quell a riot in the mines. Some forty miners were killed; the government being wholly cowed by the public's indignation, was easily deposed by the real architects of the massacre.

Assassination is not always a necessary feature of usurpation. Indeed, even though most Latin American governments emerge and disappear in a coup d'état, no state in that part of the world has had more presidents assassinated than the U.S. has. The Latin American conspirator, usually firing his weapons for the first time *after* the battle is won to celebrate victory, has become a stock character in our political cartoons. But does the cartoonist really understand that Latin American restraint stems from the same serious considerations which led the Russians to leave Dubcek alive in Czechoslovakia?

Contemporary usurpers, unlike earlier ones, usually avoid assassination. The difference is explained less by our superior humanity and intelligence than by our different conception of public office. During the Empire every Roman usurpation involved at least one assassination, for the Romans could not distinguish between the Emperor and the office he held; and since no emperor could resign, all allegiances were binding until he was dead. Later, in the Byzantine and Moslem worlds, a rudimentary distinction between office-holder and the office was understood. By maiming a ruler, one made him ineligible to hold office and simultaneously dissolved all oaths of allegiance. Since many would rather risk death than finish their lives as cripples, assassination remained a common though not a necessary feature of usurpation. In the Ottoman empire a deposed Sultan always retained an unrenounceable claim to the throne as a member of the Ottoman house. But he could consent to be imprisoned — a precaution which the Janissaries thought wise since the empire was inconceivable if the house were to be extinguished. Compared to their counterparts in the Roman, Byzantine, and Arab worlds, fewer Ottoman Sultans were assassinated; by the same token usurpers lost less blood in conspiracies because the concept of the rulers' office reduced everyone's personal stakes.

In medieval Europe political concepts for the first time became sufficiently precise to grasp the distinction between a man and his office. We have developed the implications of medieval thought to a point where personal stakes are as limited as they can possibly be and have, therefore, unwittingly maximized opportunities for bloodless usurpations. Resignation now is a complete renunciation of all formal claims, and if usurpers are willing, members of a deposed government can become private citizens, at liberty to remain in the country or leave it as they see fit.

The Romans created their obligation by direct personal oaths to the Emperor. His death created an enormous vacuum, and as various candidates received oaths of allegiance in far parts of the empire, enormous bloodbaths were required to resolve the pledges taken. We swear fealty to an entire constitution; and when a government yields, the normal constitutional bodies for designating successions may be left intact. Thus the National Assembly appointed de Gaulle, the military conspirators' choice, as Premier when the next-to-last government of the Fourth Republic resigned, legally obliging every member of the public in the process.

Nineteenth-century Spain perfected the art of bloodless usurpation — could any Roman have understood the conceptual subtleties which made Sir Henry Maine's description of Spanish politics possible?

> King Alfonso was placed on the throne . . . [in] 1874. It is generally thought that he owes his retention of it since 1875 to statesmanship of a novel kind. As soon as he assures himself that the army is in earnest, he changes his ministers.

Modern approximations of the Roman experience do exist. Hitler made German officers swear a personal unconditional oath to himself, leading German conspirators to assume that officers would remain true as long as Hitler was alive. Trujillo in the Dominican Republic, Franco in Spain, and Duvalier in Haiti exacted similar oaths. But unlike the Romans we do understand the idea of resignation. In principle, therefore, the situations are different though in particular instances they may seem identical.

The object of a usurpation is to separate individuals from their offices, replacing them with men the usurpers believe acceptable. The intelligent plotter, therefore, considers killing in expediential terms. There are always good personal reasons to avoid killing. If men have been killed and the usurpation still fails, the chances that the plotters will be executed afterwards will be increased. Even if the conspiracy is successful there is always a possibility that the new government may be ousted by a counter-insurrection, and the treatment afforded your predecessor might be cited against you — a contingency that no one living in a conspiracy-prone state forgets easily. Nor will the usurpers' anxieties cease when they retire from the political scene. In 1950 the exiled Syrian general Hinnawi was murdered in Lebanon by a cousin of the man the general had assassinated in his own quick rise to power several years before. The rule in underdeveloped countries today is that conspirators make mutual pledges beforehand not to assassinate. Hence, a president who understands how much conspirators desire to reduce their own personal risks can frustrate plots by giving unmistakable signs that he would rather forfeit his life than yield. Betancourt of Venezuela a few years ago carried a pistol conspicuously in his hip pocket, symbolizing his determination to hang on, a fact which contributed greatly to his remarkable feat of being the first elected president in that unhappy land to finish his term!

It is clear that in every phase of a usurpation attempt the chances for failure are multiplied if assassination is contemplated. During the preparation period it will be more difficult to recruit the conspirators wanted, and the possibilities of betrayal — always the major danger — will be increased. During the phase when the usurpers are actually striking, resistance is more likely. The conflict may be broadened, setting in motion wholly unanticipated forces. When younger officers assassinated Nigeria's premier during that country's first coup d'état attempt, senior officers were able to exploit the reaction immediately to stage a counter-coup. Naturally, more experienced military conspirators develop a special distaste for assassination because assassination could expand the conflict to a point where "brothers in uniform" may be compelled to fire on each other.

Finally, during the consolidation period assassination could appall foreign states whose responses might prevent new fledgling regimes from securing themselves. Recognition can be withheld, encouraging domestic opposition and bringing a junta to its knees. (On the other hand recognition must be granted when governments publicly resign.) Occasionally foreign countries have directly intervened, when heads of state are murdered, as the U.S. did when President Madeira of Mexico was assassinated. If assassination leads to serious fighting, the pressure for intervention will grow, especially if the safety of foreign nationals thereby is jeopardized.

In most cases when the prevailing conception of office does not require assassination, usurpers would be well-advised to restrain themselves. Many potential resisters will be confused and unwilling to take personal risks if they see any evidence that the usurpers will not punish without appropriate legal authority, and in the early stages of insurrection those who do not resist actually aid the rebels.

Unfortunately, the situation does not always permit restraint. Sometimes assassinations occur contrary to explicit orders, as when Diem was assassinated in South Vietnam by officers driven by hate and fear. Similarly, in Nigeria's initial series of coups and counter-coups, many were butchered because tribal animosities could not be contained. Sometimes, too, the government confounds expectation and successfully organizes resistance. If conspirators do not withdraw they must either run the risk of civil war or kill key officials — an action which could trigger the very conflict they wish to avoid. The problem is that if conspirators do not correctly anticipate the government's reaction beforehand and assassinate the most important persons before the latter begin organizing resistance, it will be too late to do so afterwards. The conspirators who attempted to topple the French Fifth Republic had no opportunities to reach de Gaulle after he issued the call for Frenchmen to fight back.

French plotters initially may have doubted de Gaulle's will or capacity to fight, but virtually all English conspirators in the 16th and 17th centuries presumed that success was impossible without the sovereign's being assassinated first. At least the scripts for so many English plots always seemed to be written by the same writer. First, kill the king, and in the subsequent confusions the insurrections prepared in various parts of the kingdom would provide a context for foreign states to intervene. Unlike the French who conspired against de Gaulle, and desperately wanted to avoid civil war, the English conspirators aimed to bring one on. The Gunpowder, or Guy Fawkes, Plot represents the most ambitious effort; in one blast King and Parliament would be blown up together, depriving the realm of all its most able leaders.

Would the insurrection have been successful if a match had been thrown into the cellars of Parliament? It is difficult to tell. No one knows the strength of Catholic sentiment in England at that time since a good many Englishmen, including most of the conspirators themselves, celebrated Mass only in secret. In situations where many have cause to distinguish between public profession and private sentiment, usurpations will be encouraged and miscalculations incurred. One thing is clear; the Gunpowder Plot significantly contributed to the long persistence of English hostility towards Catholics. Parenthetically, it is interesting to note that of the thirty or forty conspiracies attempted in this period the only two which succeeded — the one which toppled the Commonwealth in 1660, and the Glorious Revolution which brought James II down in 1688 — were organized by men who decided to avoid assassination.

A rather feeble re-enactment of the Gunpowder Plot occurred in the 19th century. The "Cato Street Conspirators" attempted to blow up the whole British Cabinet in one series of explosions. But unlike their 17th-century predecessors they believed that an insurrection would follow spontaneously, and the only effort they made to secure its success was to stockpile arms.

If conspirators think killing is necessary to secure their government but not absolutely essential to overthrowing the existing one, the question remaining is *when* to kill. Murders committed during the insurrections can be justified on grounds that the officials resisted the insurgents — a powerful justification but one which will only be accepted if it is indeed clear that the victims had been given opportunities to resign. Should the usurpers want to wait and keep their options open, other problems will ensue.

Holding officials as captives is dangerous. Those who aim at a coup d'état have very limited forces which cannot be easily spared, especially in the early moments of the strike. Even if the forces are available, there is always the possibility of escape and a renewal of the conflict — witness the examples of Charles I, Mussolini, Peron, and Lumumba. Even if the prisoner does not escape, as long as he remains alive he furnishes hope to his supporters; that is one reason why eventually most imprisoned leaders are executed. If the prisoner is not given a trial, he may become a martyr. But if allowed to defend himself in a court of law he may either escape punishment or generate public sympathy. If the government compels the court to convict regardless of the defendant's case, the judicial process will be degraded — no small matter to a new government wishing to gain popular confidence after having accused its predecessor of violating the principles of the constitution. Moreover, as the executions of Charles I, Louis XVI, and Premier Menderes of Turkey indicate, a government may find itself compelled to put men to death for actions which were never crimes when those men held offices. The resentment ensuing could persist for generations.

Usurpers ride the tiger's back: any decision involves enormous dangers. These risks may be mastered: they often are, but a sensible person would avoid taking them *if* he could.

Nowadays, usurpers commonly dispose of the problem by making certain that important personalities leave the country. In some states — Ethiopia under Haile Selassie, Ghana under President Nkrumah, Libya under King Idris, and Cambodia under Prince Sihanouk — coups d'état have been timed to coincide with the ruler's trip abroad. The intention is to dispose of two problems simultaneously — resistance and assassination or judicial murder. But Haile Selassie lived up to his title, the "Lion of Judah", by taking the next plane back, whereupon the conspirators fell all over each other to lay down their arms. The Lion of Judah is a rare phenomenon. Most moderns resemble Nkrumah more — never certain of their right to command, they are not willing to risk their lives directly. From a safe sanctuary abroad they prefer to provide a rallying point for the discontented. But if they prove too irritating, usurpers might deal with them in the manner Stalin chose for Trotsky.

One obvious difficulty with organizing coups d'état when a ruler is abroad is that he can always claim that he has never resigned his office. Latin American conspirators, whose experiences have taught them to be sensitive about the potential legal and political implications of such situations, circumvent the problem by incorporating two standard details in their plots. A resignation document is drawn up, and when the signature is obtained, the ex-President is whisked off before he can change his mind to a waiting plane destined frequently for some European pleasure resort. In the overwhelming number of cases the resignation destroys the official's prestige, although occasionally someone like Peron remains a serious political threat anyways. In some Latin American states, notably Ecuador, deposed Presidents have been permitted to return and have managed either to foment conspiracies or win elections to reap their revenge. It should be emphasized that it took the Latin Americans some time before they could fully understand the great range of possibilities implicit in the modern conception of office. For the first half-century of their existence, like African states today, assassination seemed to be practised much more often than "necessary".

In the West, when heredity determined right to office and the allegiance of subjects was to a house or dynasty, the problems of the usurper could be much more difficult and persist for longer periods of time. By compelling a monarch to abdicate, one merely opened the way to other members of the house. But if the king were permitted merely to go into exile, he was free to seek help from other royal houses related to him by blood or marriage, and his sons, grandsons, and great-grandsons in turn could seek aid. Machiavelli, therefore, insisted that all members of the ruling house be killed. Whether the solution was practical or not, it does suggest a problem peculiar to dynasties. The British were forced to wrestle with various Stuart Pretenders for sixty-three years before the Battle of Culloden settled the issue once and for all in 1745. Even today the laws of Austria forbid a Habsburg, and those of Germany a Hohenzollern, from even visiting their former realms.

Let me sum up the contemporary situation as a potential usurper might see it. His purpose is to separate individuals from their offices, making sure that they are in no position to reclaim them. He, therefore, has three alternatives. Imprisonment for an indefinite period without trial is the least preferred course because it involves too many risks. Assassination is more common, but still one is struck by how rarely it occurs, especially when the enormous stakes of the game are considered and a comparison with previous periods is made. More usurpers prefer to try their opponents in court, but the largest proportion allow them to go free, especially if they can be induced to leave the country. If officials are permitted to reside in their homeland, usurpers must first strip them of their offices. An elementary consideration this seems, but one often violated. Those who organized the Kapp Putsch in Germany during the Weimar Republic were so contemptuous of President Ebert that they allowed him to leave the capital without resigning, whereupon he used his powers to organize the resistance which finally defeated them. Hitler made the same miscalculation when he organized the Beer Hall Putsch. Surrounding the assembled notables of Bavaria with his armed followers, he exacted a sworn promise to support him before yielding to their demands for release. When they later ordered his arrest, he discovered that they were not gentlemen. In prison, unfortunately, he had more time to reflect on the techniques of usurpation.

ASSASSINATIONS ORGANIZED BY GOVERNMENTS AND THE TERRORIST MENTALITY

Today I shall conclude the discussion of assassination plots, and then take up the question of terrorism.

Assassination must always be considered a desperate gambler's stroke; but the risks are reduced sometimes when government is associated with the attempt — a type of plot I have not yet discussed. Obviously assassins protected by a government interested in eliminating a domestic rival find it easier to get to their victim and to escape afterwards. A government which controls its administrative apparatus is in a good position to contain the potential political backlash also. Still, the dangers of a public's fury are so great that most governments are at pains to conceal their role.

The enterprise becomes much more hazardous when a government intrigues against a neighbor. The risk appears worth taking whenever power in a foreign state is highly personalized and a sizeable portion of its population seems sympathetic to the plotters' cause. Thus in the West assassins became conventional instruments of foreign policy for the first time during the Reformation, when the power of princes rose to unprecedented levels while religious conflicts simultaneously flowed across state borders. Every Canadian schoolboy knows that Spanish kings believed that Englishmen would have the courage to reveal their secret Catholic sympathies when their own sovereign was no longer able to punish them. Similarly, plots are common today in underdeveloped countries where one-man government is the rule and where it appears that loyalties may go to persons or parties based in other states. Egypt, Ghana, Cuba, and many others have frequently intrigued against particularly vulnerable neighbors.

The strategy, a "fifth column strategy", can work when the isolated column (the potential sympathizers) expects the other four columns (the conventional armies of the intriguing states) to march to its aid immediately; but the irony is that just *because* intriguers cannot employ conventional military means, they often become attracted to assassination! After the defeat of the Armada prevented Spanish troops from invading England, Spanish plots became more numerous than ever before. The same pattern has been occurring in underdeveloped states as the ineptitude of the armies available became clearer, and in both the Reformation and modern instances plots have simply given the intended victim remarkable opportunities to crush the potential fifth column.

Generally assassination is the tactic of the resourceless, those who risk much believing that they have little to lose and no alternatives. But whereas in domestic politics it is most often the weak who assassinate the strong, plot patterns in the international world are strikingly different. Weak governments understand that they cannot topple strong neighbors with assassins, and that they may provoke massive retaliation. The weak, therefore, generally plot against those too weak to hit back, except perhaps by organizing assassinations themselves.

A government which cannot pursue foreign policy by conventional means and uses assassins instead, is also likely to be a government so vulnerable that its weapons perform like boomerangs in the hands of the inexperienced. Note Nkrumah's pathetic tale. Accusations that he had masterminded the assassination of President Olympio in Togoland caused support in that country to vanish. Bitter denunciations by the leaders of the African "Third Force" states then destroyed his dominance in that group. Finally these events helped undermine his domestic prestige, especially among Ghanian officers who ultimately deposed him.

All governments seek to conceal their assassination plots. The extraordinary case of the Republic of Venice in the 16th and 17th centuries indicates how successful they may be sometimes. When the state archives were opened 200 years later, dumbfounded historians learned that the Republic had paid for several hundred assassination attempts. Only a few plots succeeded, and often she was swindled by confidence men masquerading as assassins. Her experience, incidentally, demonstrates a principal theme in Jack London's novel, *The Assassination Bureau Ltd.* If you desperately want to conceal your role in a plot, hire assassins to "arrange accidents" or administer poison; but, alas, the Venetian archives show quite clearly that the methods best calculated to conceal the plotter's identity so complicate the plot that they simultaneously multiply possibilities that the victim will escape too — a problem that even Jack London failed to appreciate.

Assassination attempts are generally desperate gambler's strokes. Strong states do not fear the weak and have more reliable means to impose their will. Even against other strong states they prefer to use means whose effects are easier to control. So suspicious are strong states of assassins that they will not generally gamble with them even in the desperate circumstances of war. There obviously are military occasions when assassinations might serve a useful purpose, such as when a large element of the enemy's population is opposed to the conflict and able to seize the opportunity provided to make its opposition more effective. The problem is that assassins might provoke the one reaction feared most. If Hanoi's agents attempted to assassinate the U.S. President, the public might be angry enough to support a bigger military commitment. Similarly, if the U.S. sent assassination teams against Hanoi's leaders, the reaction among her allies in the Communist world might prolong and intensify the conflict further. In most wars belligerents lack sufficient justification to commit their full resources. And just as the demand for unconditional surrender provides an opponent with powerful justification because he does not know our intentions and fears the worst, so assassination attempts generally provoke a will to fight harder without supplying sufficient gains in return. If the listener has any doubts, I would ask him to study the experience of the Reformation.

When resources are fully committed because both sides understand their struggle as a life-death one, it may make sense to assassinate the enemy's leaders when they are clearly superior to our own. Hannibal was incomparably the greatest soldier of his day, and the Romans rightly reckoned his life to be worth several armies. But organizing assassination teams from abroad during war is extremely difficult business, and it is no surprise that the Roman attempts failed.

Parenthetically, it should be emphasized that judging the value of a live leader is tricky business. No evidence is more compelling than his previous successes, but spectacular successes can easily corrupt critical faculties. The case of the Nazis is notorious. In difficult situations when his generals advised caution, Hitler always gambled on the more adventurous course. Until the invasion of Russia Hitler's gambling impulses paid rich dividends, and his confidence in the German generals' counsel (indeed their confidence in their own advice) waned. Later Hitler's gambles misfired; but the generals could not prevail, so well established was his credit. Had Hitler been assassinated in 1942, the Germans might have knocked Russia out of the war; certainly they would have made fewer costly military mistakes. The end of Napoleon's career suggests a similar deterioration. The legend is that at Waterloo a young officer came rushing up to Wellington to report that the Corsican's tent was within shell range. But Wellington ordered the guns turned around, believing that the French would be easier to beat with him alive.

To use assassins effectively during the war the preliminary work must be done in peace. But once it becomes known that a state dispatches assassins, she may be blamed for assassinations organized by others. In the wake of President Kennedy's assassination the American government's most pressing problem was to convince itself and then its people that no foreign power was responsible. Imagine the problems if a potential enemy had had a widespread reputation for employing assassins. Even today most Americans who do not find the Warren Report credible believe that in some way a foreign power was implicated, and the majority of those who do subscribe to this view think that Castro's government was the culprit, partly because of her reputation for fomenting plots to assassinate Latin American presidents. Prudence suggests one final reason for eschewing assassins in war. As soon as one state begins to prepare during peace for assassination in war, other states obviously will follow suit. The most effective assassins will be high-ranking officials in the enemy's government or security forces. A climate of mistrust will develop between members of the same government whose short- and long-run consequences for every citizen could be disastrous.

I have only discussed some major aspects of assassination, and while I would like to develop the arguments further, the constraints on time make it necessary to turn now to the second subject of the series — terrorism. For the remainder of the talk today I will compare the assassin with the terrorist. Next time I will discuss terrorist movements.

There is a close relationship between the assassin and the terrorist. The law generally does not distinguish between them because both deliver sneak attacks on defenseless persons who have not offered the assailant a personal offense. The Society of Assassins, the Ismaili in medieval Islam, is the first terrorist movement known to the Western world. A few terrorist groups in 19th-century Europe and America even acknowledged an Islamic lineage, and many more individual terrorists proudly called themselves "Assassins".

Yet there are profound differences between the assassin and the terrorist, differences which can be appreciated best by focusing on the meaning of their actions rather than on the acts themselves. In my first talk I noted that Greco-Roman and Christian cultures provided justifications for assassination. The assailant could argue that his victim was guilty of monstrous deeds or intentions; in principle the evil matters were demonstrable in a court of law but circumstances prevented the judicial process from operating properly. If, however, the assassin could not demonstrate his case or if his action lead to a worse state of affairs, he was obliged to accept punishment. In his mind the assassin destroys men who are corrupting a system while the terrorist destroys a system which has *already* corrupted everyone it touches. The vastness of this difference and the variety of ensuing consequences simply cannot be overestimated. In principle the guilt or innocence of the terrorist's victim is irrelevant. The terrorist often deliberately kills persons innocent of any wrong-doing, knowing that terror spreads more rapidly and is more paralyzing when men are murdered indiscriminately.

Assassination is an incident, a passing deed, an event; terrorism is a process, a way of life, a dedication. At most assassination involves a conspiracy, but terrorism requires a movement since fear dissipates unless the pressure continues to persist over long periods of time. In the words of the prophet Isaiah:

> When the overwhelming scourge passes,
> You will be battered down by it;
> As often as it passes, it will bear you away;
> For morning, by morning will it pass,
> Both day and night;
> And sheer terror will it be
> To understand the message.

This assassin wishes to be judged here and now by standards available to everyone. The terrorist lives in another world, which is governed by an awesome idea whose logic turns all conventional distinctions upside down. It is not contemporaries but future generations who will judge whether this victim or another should have been selected. But future generations cannot make the final judgment unless he spreads terror, and in the act of murder his name is entered on the honor roll of those who kept the faith.

Consider once again that remarkable prototype of pure terrorism — the Ismaili. Organizing the world's first political anarchist movement, they hoped to terrorize Moslems into abandoning the state. The typical Ismaili was placed in the service of a high official. By devotion and skill over a period of years he gained his master's confidence, and then in response to the cult leader's signal the faithful servant would plunge a dagger into his master's back. Generation after generation the terror continued, even though governments lashed out at innocent bystanders and the movement could get no closer to its goals. Sustaining the cult was the belief that regardless of consequences to others, the assassin always gained a place in paradise himself — a perversion, incidentally, of the ordinary Moslem doctrine that those who fell in a holy war went to heaven.

Ordinary Moslems wrestled to find an appropriate term for the Ismaili. A *fatik*, the conventional word for assassin,* did not kill personal benefactors for a bizarre cause in the hope of an implausible reward. Nor did a *fatik* seek death himself. Increasingly

---

*I am indebted to my colleague Professor Louis Cantori for helping to clarify this point.

38

Moslems called the Ismaili *hashishaya*, a drug addict, because he generally took drugs before launching his murderous assault; and more importantly because like a drug addict, he wanted to live in a world where ordinary experiences were no longer relevant.

The connection, incidentally, between certain drugs and terror has always been close. The writings of 19th-century Romantics tell us that a major effect of opium is that it induces terror — a psychological state which simultaneously attracts and repels the addict. Baudelaire's hashish cult recognized the "Old Man of the Mountain", the leader of the Ismaili, as a kind of patron saint. Before they strike the "crazies get stoned", American students gossip. The Yippie leader Jerry Rubin says that the "symbol of the Yippie-Panther Pact is a hash-pipe crossed by a gun". The Weathermen claim credit for helping Dr. Timothy Leary, the high priest of LSD, to escape from jail and join the Panthers in Algeria. A recent tape ostensibly made by Leary, and revealed by sources close to the Weathermen, argues that political revolution and drug culture need each other and concluded by advising the young, "Blow your mind and blow up the prisons and the controlling systems of the genocidal culture." And finally Dieter Kunzelman, a German Anarchist now with the Arab terrorists, has been quoted as saying:

> As for the emotional concentration of our anger, it is a matter of indifference what its sources are — even if it is a rage which derives from drugs we must be able to incorporate it.

To return to the Ismaili, who represent the most extreme case in terrorist history, no movement had a more impossible goal, none asked every assassin to murder alone while making certain that he would die himself. Indeed, the Ismaili are an extreme case, but like most extreme cases they are interesting because they manifest in a vivid fashion crucial universal tendencies and contradictions generally unnoticed in less radical instances.

Take, for example, the Ismaili belief that in the act of violence he purged *himself* of all impurities. An extraordinary claim which no assassin needs to make; and in the extensive literature justifying assassination one can hardly find a trace of it. But the argument or some variant always appears in terrorist literature, even though the secondary accounts sometimes obscure it in an eagerness to describe the social objectives of the movement.

In *The Wretched of the Earth*, a basic text of contemporary terrorism, one which has fired the imagination of so many student terrorists everywhere, Dr. Frantz Fanon tells us that one transcends his own corruption in killing:

> Violence is a purifying force. It frees the native from
> his inferiority complex and from despair and inaction.
> It makes him fearless and restores his self-respect.

A Brazilian terrorist manual declares:

> To be a terrorist is a quality that ennobles any honor-
> able man because it is an act worthy of a revolu-
> tionary.

And Menachem Begin justifies the Irgun, an Israeli terrorist movement, in language Descartes used to underscore the primacy of
reason!

> A new generation grew up which turned its back on
> fear. It began to fight instead of to plead . . . a people
> may 'think' and its sons, with their thoughts, and in
> spite of them, may be turned into soap . . . *We fight,*
> *and therefore we are* [author's stress].

The more flagrantly a particular murder offends normal sensibilities the more it excites the admiration of some people, one
reason why Bernardine Dohrn, a leader of the Weathermen
terrorist movement, finds herself stirred by those horrible Tate-La
Bianca mass murders allegedly committed by Charles Manson's
"family". "Dig it," she commands. "First they killed the pigs, then
they ate dinner in the same room with them, then they even shoved
a fork into the victim's stomach! Wild!"

The writings of Nachaeyeff, the first Russian terrorist of the
19th century, are dominated by a frenzy, a lust for destruction. No
wonder Dostoyevsky called his novel in which Nachaeyeff is the
major figure *The Possessed*. Listen to Nachaeyeff's own "Revolutionary Catechism":

> The revolutionary [terrorist] despises all dogmas and
> all sciences, leaving them for future generations. He
> knows only one science — the science of destruction
> . . . the object is perpetually the same: the quickest
> and surest way of destroying this whole filthy
> order . . . .

For him, there exists only one pleasure, one consolation, one reward, one satisfaction, the success of the terror. Night and day he must have but one thought, one aim, merciless destruction . . . .

The revolutionary enters the world . . . of the state, of the classes and of the so-called civilization, and he lives in this world only because he has faith in its quick and complete destruction. He no longer remains a revolutionary, if he keeps faith with anything in this world. He must hate *everyone*, and *everything* with *equal hatred*. All the worse for him if he has . . . relationships with parents, friends, or lovers; he is no longer a revolutionary [terrorist] if he is swayed by these relationships . . . .

The future plan of life is a matter for future generations to decide. Our task is terrible, total, inexorable, and universal destruction.

In drawing closer to the people, we must unite above all with those elements who have never ceased to protest since the foundation of the State . . . not only in words, but in deeds against everything directly and indirectly connected with the State . . . we must unite with the . . . bands of robbers, who are the only true revolutionaries of Russia.

Similar heroes and similar frenzies appear in the writings of Jerry Rubin, leader of the American Yippies:

[The killers] Bonnie & Clyde *are the leaders of the New Youth*.

All money represents theft. To steal from the rich is a sacred and religious act. To take what you need is an act of self-love, self-liberation. While looting, a man to his own self is true.

When in doubt burn. Fire is the revolutionary's god. Fire is instant theater. No words can match fire. Politicians only notice poverty when the ghettos burn . . .
Burn the flag, burn the churches

Burn, Burn, Burn [Rubin's emphasis].

All terrorists must deny the relevance of guilt and innocence, but in doing so they create an unbearable tension in their own souls, for they are in effect saying that a person is not a person. It is no accident that left-wing terrorists constantly speak of a "pig society"; by convincing *themselves* that they are confronting animals they hope to stay the remorse which the slaughter of the innocent necessarily generates. Right-wing terrorism has a similar vocabulary. Listen to the words of a Ku Klux Klan agitator trying to make Klansmen forget that one of their bombs killed four children:

> I'll tell you people here tonight, if they can find those fellows who threw the bomb, they ought to pin medals on them. Someone said, 'ain't it a shame little children was killed.' Well, they don't know what they're talking about. In the first place, they ain't little. They're 14 or 15 years old, old enough to have venereal diseases and I'll be surprised if all of them didn't have one or more. In the second place, they weren't children. Children are little people, little human beings, and that means white people. There's little monkeys, there's little dogs and little cats, little apes, little baboons, little skunks, and there's also little Niggers. They're just little Niggers. And in the third place, it wasn't no shame they was killed.

> Why? Because when I go out to kill rattlesnakes, I don't make no difference between little rattlesnakes and big rattlesnakes because I know it is in the nature of all rattlesnakes to be my enemies and to poison me if they can. So, I kill 'em all, and if there's four less little Niggers tonight, then I say, good for whoever planted the bomb. We're all better off.

Making statements of this sort is one thing; really believing them is something altogether different. Last year in New York City left-wing terrorists made frantic telephone calls pleading with occupants to abandon the buildings before the bombs went off. Student terrorism, of course, is new in America, and its practitioners are still squeamish; some are unable yet to kill real pigs, let alone men they call pigs. But even when they learn to be more steady, as they are, some will find that no matter what they do, they cannot suppress their own natural feelings and innate sense of justice. In *The Wretched of the Earth* Dr. Fanon, who was a psychiatrist, appended descriptions of patients he treated in

Algerian hospitals; all broke down, *not* because their doctrine compelled them to kill, but rather because it made them murder persons they knew to be innocent!

Next time I shall discuss the theory of modern revolutionary terrorism and the first two movements it inspired in the late 19th century. Those movements failed because their leaders confused the strategic and tactical principles appropriate to assassination with those necessary for terrorism. Twentieth-century terrorists, unfortunately, have learned to correct those mistakes.

Last time I noted that the terrorist often deliberately assails the innocent, convincing many bystanders that short of joining the terrorist they can do nothing to eliminate the *possibility* of becoming his victim, too. In maximizing uncertainty he excites extraordinary apprehensions; terror springs *less* from dangers which can be anticipated and thus prepared for, and *more* from those which are so uncertain that our imagination makes them far worse than they actually are.

In recent decades the terrorist has so often confined his activity to the city and co-operated with the guerrilla that we have slipped into the habit of calling him an urban guerrilla. But he is not really a guerrilla. In Spanish the word *guerrilla* means "little war" and the guerrilla is a little warrior. His aim is to disperse the state's conventional forces so that he may defeat them piecemeal. Because he directs his energies against military units the guerrilla has won a begrudging partial recognition in domestic and international law as a soldier himself, and is entitled to the privileges and immunities of that status when captured. The terrorist is not a soldier and prefers to avoid military targets. Recently, for example, Arab terrorists lying in ambush let several clearly marked Israeli military vehicles pass to destroy a bus loaded with schoolchildren. Their purpose was to provoke Israelis into murdering Arab children in Israel which in turn might induce an Arab uprising. When the terrorist does attack soldiers, he goes out of his way to kill in the most bizarre fashion, and he mutilates prisoners or employs them as hostages; that is one reason why courts treat terrorists as criminals.

Our law primarily deals with actions; and from the perspective of the law a terrorist is only one who violates particular conventions regulating civil or military intercourse. But to understand the terrorist properly we must keep his *purpose* in mind, and from *his* perspective the true terrorist is destroying conventions to demonstrate that there are no immunities, no restraints worth respecting. Ultimately, he wants his antagonist to respond in kind, for without conventions no social relationship is possible.

A true terrorist *consciously* employs terror, believing that the end desired cannot be produced in any other way. When the Germans dropped booby traps attached to children's toys on Britain in 1940, they were using terror tactics, hoping to terrify those who could fight by slaughtering those who could not — the most innocent, the most defenseless, and the most loved. But the Germans were not true terrorists, because when it became clear that the tactic was counterproductive they returned to more traditional military means. The scalp of a woman or child gave the North American brave honor, and when the white man said that the only good Indian was a dead one he was responding to the Indian's fighting methods, responding as most people do when confronted by those whom they regard as terrorists. But again the Indian was not a true terrorist; he knew no other way of fighting, was not sufficiently conscious of his practices to change them, either by repudiating terror or alternatively by making it more efficient!

From the beginning of time we have experienced terror tactics. But a terrorist campaign, the prolonged, systematic use of terror to secure a political objective, is, by comparison, conspicuously rare, and the true terrorist enters history late. The first clear example is the Ismaili in medieval Islam. European civilization produced its first terrorist movement in the late 18th century, and the number of instances since have continually multiplied, until today a bewildered anxious newspaper reader might be forgiven for thinking that virtually every existing state must have had at least one important terrorist experience to record.

For the rest of the series I shall concentrate on some of these terror campaigns, particularly those associated with revolutionary insurrections, to illustrate common features and problems. My topics today are the logic of modern terrorism as it was first developed in the 19th century. Next time, which will be the last time, we shall discuss subsequent modifications in strategy and doctrine.

The first two examples of *successful* terrorist campaigns were fought in the U.S. The "Sons of Liberty" during the War for Independence compelled a sizeable minority to support the struggle against Britain or face the consequences (many listeners tonight, in fact, may be descendants of those who settled in Canada as a consequence). Nearly a century later American terrorists led by the "Ku Klux Klan" were successful again, this time salvaging something from the defeat of Confederate armies by compelling the Federal government to terminate the occupation and frustrate the plans of the radical Republicans.

Neither the Sons of Liberty nor the Klan tried to explain their success or develop an explicit logic for terror; one might say that they did their dirty work in secret and kept their mouths shut, for they inspired no significant imitators. The lineage of modern terrorism, therefore, does not originate in America but in 19th-century Russia where writers sketched a doctrine proclaiming the virtue of terror, suggesting the type of society vulnerable to it, and indicating appropriate strategic principles. Ironically, those who first made the logic of terror public bungled badly in their attempt to apply it.

When a mistrustful peasantry seemed unaware that it was oppressed, how could one begin a revolution? This was the question dividing Russian intellectuals. The debate, it should be stressed, was not over whether Tsarist Russia permitted men to speak to each other freely about the need for revolution but more fundamentally over how to gain the peasant's confidence. Most revolutionaries took a pedestrian, commonsense position, believing that they ought to live among the peasants, share their burdens, explain the oppressive nature of the system and the appropriate solution, a process which might require generations. But the minority argued that revolution involved such a profound transformation in human consciousness that a special dramatic way to realize it was required. In living among peasants revolutionaries would inevitably become like them — timid, vascillating, and perpetually willing to compromise the cause for the sake of immediate short-run advantages. Even if this did not happen, could peasants place faith in a revolutionary's commitment knowing that whenever village life depressed the revolutionary he could return to the city? Bold action alone would establish the revolutionary's credit, action which would demonstrate a completely unconditional and irrevocable opposition to the existing order.

Nachaeyeff called such action "propaganda of the deed", a phrase which student terrorists everywhere nowadays use so freely. Existing revolutionary societies, he charged, were composed of "idle word spillers" circulating pamphlets which only other revolutionaries, who spend their lives reading and talking, take. The public knows that revolutionaries *do* nothing, and even revolutionaries suspect themselves as being nothing but worthless dissemblers. Let a revolutionary finally *act* in a spectacular fashion; he will regain his self-respect and find himself performing before a huge audience composed of people very different from those who used to take his pamphlets. Dramatize the cause, prove that someone is willling to risk everything for it, and a series of actions and reactions will occur which ultimately will inflame all the hatreds smouldering in society.

An intrepid revolutionary excites admiration, attracts followers, and inspires emulators. But since the number of bold spirits in any society must always be extremely small, they cannot induce a revolution without the unwitting complicity of government. By employing terror against officials, the revolutionaries will so thoroughly panic a government that it will lash out indiscriminately against those it cannot find, making the oppression of the masses so visible that a revolutionary insurrection is inevitable. The strategy of the revolutionary terrorist, in other words, is to attack the masses, the very people he wants to liberate, but to attack them in such a way that it is the government which appears to be their enemy. Nachaeyeff writes:

> The aims of our Society are . . . the entire emancipation and happiness of the people . . . . Convinced that their emancipation and the achievement of this happiness is brought about only by means of an all-destroying popular revolt, we shall see that [government] will employ all its power, all its resources towards increasing the people's calamities and evils until their patience is exhausted and they will break out in a *levée-en-masse*.

A century later, despite our greater familiarity with terrorist activity, Nachaeyeff's simple description of the fundamental strategic principle still seems too bizarre to be credible. But Russians familiar with their government's Balkan intrigues during the early 19th century were hardly surprised. The Tsars themselves had used assassins against Turkish officials, who responded by massacring local Christians, which in turn created both a demand among those Christians for Russian intervention and a war fever in Russia itself. Nachaeyeff's proposal embodied the same principle; the real question was whether the additional practical difficulties in executing it were insuperable.

The classic revolutionary sees society deeply divided by openly hostile classes with unequal shares of wealth. Without this condition he will not attempt insurrection. Nachaeyeff speaks not of a divided society but a *corrupt* one — not social structure but individual attitudes are the terrorist's true fuel. In the corrupt society most men are fundamentally ambivalent about their commitments. Dissatisfactions are so diffused and concealed that one is not fully conscious even of his own feelings, let alone anyone else's, and the normal activities of society are reasonably well conducted. Few are desperately unhappy, but everyone has grievances and most are too deeply involved in day-to-day responsibilities to imagine alternatives. The few who really want revolution *now* feel isolated and discouraged because the hostility to the system they sense everywhere lacks direction and even appears shallow. But people are attached to the system because it provides personal amenities — peace and security — and they are extremely vulnerable; their perpetual recriminations indicate that they are guilt-ridden, intimidated by wild men who act out all the fantasies of the guilty. Terrorism supplies the first group — those who want revolution *now* — with hope, inspiration, and direction; and terrorism intimidates the second group, the ambivalent guilt-ridden ones, by impaling them on their own consciences and then depriving them of peace and security, so that they must ask themselves what it is that they want and what dangers would they be willing to endure to secure it.

The great movements in history are not class achievements but generational ones. Creative epochs are succeeded by corrupt ones which in turn stimulate the appetite for destruction. The more devastating the destruction the grander the opportunities for those to come; and Nachaeyeff's generation was the first to be fully conscious of its destiny, of its obligation: "terrible, total, complete destruction. . . . Aiming cold-bloodedly and untiringly towards this, [the terrorist] must be ready to destroy himself and destroy with his own hands everyone who stands in his way." The form life will take tomorrow is wholly the concern of the next generation; a terrorist who tries to imagine its character will succeed in diverting his energies from the only role history will allow him to play — that of supreme executioner.

To complement his social diagnosis Nachaeyeff began to develop the organization and tactics appropriate for a terrorist movement, but before he finished he was imprisoned for murdering one of his own comrades, the chief dramatic event, incidentally, for Dostoyevsky's novel *The Possessed*. But Nachaeyeff did not lose his influence. In 1879 *Narodnaya Volya* — "The Will of the People" — was born. Its announced program was "to liquidate the worst officials — to give constant proof that it is possible to fight the government, to strengthen the revolutionary spirit of the people and its faith in the success of the cause, and finally to form capable cadres trained in the struggle". *Narodnaya Volya's* strategy involved two quick tactical steps: first, assassinate a number of crucial officials, the last and most important being the Tsar, who was considered the lynchpin of the system; and secondly when the Tsar was dead the masses would rise. *Narodnaya Volya* saw a necessity to have months elapse between each murder and to have them done publicly so that the terror would have its full effect; otherwise the plan seemed designed by one of the English conspirators of the 17th century who thought the assassination of the king would touch off an insurrection. The resemblance is not surprising since the English conspirators and Russian terrorists presumed a similar society, one where men said one thing in public and another in private. The English failed and the Russians succeeded in their first step. After seven attempts against him Alexander II was literally blown apart, but still no revolution occurred. In the end the Russian terrorists, like their English predecessors, were virtually all apprehended; only three of the thirty-six members of the First Executive Committee were able to flee the country. The organization was active for only two years.

New Russian terrorist movements sprang up to replace *Narodnaya Volya*, but it seemed clear that terrorism had reached its high-water mark with the assassination of Alexander II. The masses grew hostile to revolutionaries and even reformers of all sorts. And soon most of the revolutionaries condemned the terrorists too as infantile adventurers. Catholic conspiracies made England more thoroughly Protestant, and terror only seemed to strengthen the Tsars' hand.

The assassination of Alexander II had a different, radical, and immediate effect in Europe and America, inspiring the most spectacular terrorist exploits in the history of Western civilization. For almost three decades one major minister was assassinated every eighteen months, and the number of minor officials murdered in some countries like Spain was so great that to my knowledge no accurate tally has ever been compiled. Britain alone, among the major powers, seemed immune, that is, if we ignore Ireland and forget that British residents fashioned a pipe-line for funds and explosives to terrorists abroad.

In Western Europe the terrorist's immediate aim was to destroy the drive towards universal suffrage, believing that if radicals were compelled to solicit votes they would emasculate the purity of their program by catering to the immediate desires of their constituents. If universal suffrage were truly in the interest of the people, the terrorist asked, would a Louis Napoleon or a Bismarck have dared to introduce the principle in their countries? No, the electoral process operated to conceal hostilities, heighten ambivalence, and deflect the revolution; hence the strategic principle in the West was the same as it had been in Russia — panic government into adopting a policy of indiscriminate repression.

But if the strategic problem was the same, the terrorists' striking or tactical patterns were different, a difference which stemmed from the contrasting political character of the two terrorist movements. Although profoundly influenced by Nachaeyeff, *Narodnaya Volya* consisted primarily of liberals with the mundane aim of bringing parliamentary government to Russia, linked in a single conspiratorial organization to co-ordinate tactics systematically. The terrorists of western Europe and America, on the other hand, were Anarchists, inspired by Bakunin, an elder associate of Nachaeyeff, aiming at total destruction. The logic of Anarchism demanded that terrorists work as individuals or in small wholly independent units choosing targets without any direction from above. In refusing to create an organization, the Anarchists made it more difficult for the police to cope; the terror was more profound than in Russia, involving more assassins, more officials, and more citizens.

Nonetheless the results seemed similar. The climate for all radicals in the West grew more chilly, and everywhere radicals angrily turned on the terrorists. When Lenin, whose elder brother was a terrorist killed by the Tsar's police, explained why terrorism must always fail, he was expressing a view which became more and more popular among radicals everywhere in the early part of our century:

> It would be difficult to imagine an argument more obviously self-refuting. Are there so few crying abuses ... that one must invent 'special irritants' .... Those who are neither excited nor excitable at the sight of despotism will sit by and twiddle their thumbs when a handful of terrorists battle with government.

But the epitaph was written too soon. Perhaps every government the terrorists attacked was too strong to be brought down, but it is quite certain that the Russian and Western terrorists provided a very poor show. They did not make the most of their opportunities; one could learn from their mistakes, and there were situations in which terrorism could be almost as destructive as Nachaeyeff had hoped.

From our vantage point in time it is easy to list the many avoidable difficulties the terrorists created for themselves, difficulties which Nachaeyeff had anticipated and warned his comrades about. Two of the more conspicuous capital blunders pertained to organization and tactics. Not willing to recognize that a successful terrorist movement must prepare for a long ordeal and organize itself accordingly, *Narodnaya Volya* concentrated all its strength in one body to deliver several quick knockout blows; after an initial success or two it was, like a typical 17th-century assassination conspiracy, penetrated by the police and easily crushed. Western European and American terrorists were more destructive and demonstrated more staying power, but without an organization their movements could not be co-ordinated.

No one considered the immense possibilities of Nachaeyeff's ingenious organizational plan of tiny virtually independent cells governed primarily by general directives to maximize flexibility, initiative, and invulnerability. Each cell would have direct links only to two others, one below and one above it, and each separate link would be maintained by one person who belonged to both cells; in this way the process of police penetration would be persistently slowed, providing opportunities for effective countermeasures. The success of the three-man Vietcong and four-man Algerian terrorist cell teams superbly illustrates the force of Nachaeyeff's suggestion, and virtually all terrorist movements from the IRA to the FLQ and Weathermen have utilized this principle or some variant.

Obsessed with their own hatred and their dream to perform spectacular exploits quickly, the early terrorists failed to realize that it takes time and continuous effort to develop whatever latent hostilities a people possess. Preaching terrorism they actually practised 17th-century tyrannicide. The point is obvious in the Russian case because of the ridiculous importance attached to the Tsar's murder, but even in western Europe and America, where no single comparable target existed, terrorists acted as though every official was already regarded by the public as a tyrant. Murdering major officials only makes political sense when the public can accept the deeds as justified reactions to governmental excesses. Otherwise, the dramatic appeal of assassination will be as fatal to the terrorists as the light of a flame is to a moth.

Before his imprisonment, Nachaeyeff had written that hated officials should be kept alive until they served the terrorist's purpose fully. But shortly afterwards when *Narodnaya Volya* announced its program, "liquidating the worst officials" had top priority, "inspiring revolutionary fervor" second, and "forming capable cadres trained in the struggle" last. Clearly no terrorist campaign was ever more confused about the correct priorities, and none seemed more obviously fated for disaster. One can only imagine that the intoxication with the idea of murder — an inherent terrorist vice — was having its full effect. Even Nachaeyeff, when faced with a practical decision, ignored his own writings.

Learning that *Narodnaya Volya* had strength only either to storm his prison or assassinate the Tsar, he sent word that the Tsar must die, apparently thinking that all the Tsar's prisons would collapse with his death.

Generally modern terrorists have followed the advice of the earlier rather than the later Nachaeyeff. The Vietcong did not assassinate Diem. Castro spurned all offers to assassinate Batista, recognizing that since he was too weak to dictate a successor, the new government would get a fresh supply of credit and be in a better position to stop the Revolution. Castro was not a terrorist, but in the initial stages of an insurrection launched by the weak the paramount concern must always be to build one's own strength *first*.

In my talk next time I will discuss the development of modern terrorist tactics, show the distinct stages in a terrorist campaign, and indicate a few of the conditions shaping success or failure.

Last time I discussed the genesis of the modern revolutionary terrorist doctrine and the first two movements it inspired during the late 19th and early 20th centuries. Today my focus is on more recent developments.

The early movements failed partly because they would not or could not follow Nachaeyeff's advice on appropriate organizations and tactics. Driven by their own lust for murder, the terrorists mounted spectacular attacks against prominent persons. A prominent person, however, can be guarded well; in such circumstances assassins must be willing to exchange their lives for the ones they take, and no modern terrorist movement has enough willing members for many such undertakings.

Terrorism always involves spectacular feats; that is why it attracts the very young whose thirst for notoriety makes them believe Jerry Rubin's adage that "History [can] be changed in a day. An hour. A second." Weakness compels the terrorist to deliver spectacular blows, but that same weakness makes it impossible to risk many casualties, for few terrorist groups number more than several hundred. The modern terrorist, therefore, seeks relatively defenseless targets and tries to develop qualities which enable him to survive again and again, qualities which are quite rare among young men obsessed with hate — qualities of patience and judgment.

A correct terrorist strategy aims to avoid battles, to destroy a system by maddening and frightening its defenders into wearing themselves out in vain efforts to find an enemy who is everywhere in general but nowhere in particular, an enemy who seems to grow constantly stronger. All this requires time, much more time than even Nachaeyeff realized. The terror must go on and on until all the assets of the constitutional order disintegrate.

Most of the more recent developments in terror as an insurrectional doctrine and tactic originated in former colonial territories such as Macedonia, Ireland, Israel, Algeria, Cyprus, and Vietnam. Let me emphasize that despite numerous attempts no system has yet been overturned by terror alone; even Nachaeyeff did not claim that one could be. The campaign in Cyprus represents the most complete modern terrorist success so far; the result, incidentally, is comparable to that produced by the Ku Klux Klan a century ago. Without the aid of guerrillas Cypriot terrorists forced British troops to withdraw, but the real objective — union with Greece — was never achieved.

In every case where modern terrorists have been successful, they have been associated with organized military forces, especially guerrillas. Normally the terrorist precedes the guerrilla or creates the political context where guerrilla action becomes possible. But in Algeria a terrorist movement was formed to revive the flagging fortunes of badly harassed guerrilla bodies. When Abane Ramdane began the reign of terror in Algiers he asked:

> Which is better for our cause? To kill ten enemies in a gulch in the country — which will go unnoticed, or one in Algiers which will be written up the next day in the American press? If we are going to risk our lives, we must make our struggle known. We could kill hundreds of colonialist soldiers without even making news.

A well-planned terrorist campaign to provoke revolution develops in three clearly marked phases. In the first period the organization prepares, then it initiates attacks to secure momentum and encourage latent hostilities, and finally it takes the struggle out of the government's hands and crushes liberal or moderating elements hoping to secure a political solution which all can accept. Obviously, in all phases cells are organized and hostilities developed, and an assassination of a moderate may occur; but both logic and experience indicate that successful terrorists devote the bulk of their energies to the task appropriate for each phase. How quickly each phase will be completed depends upon circumstances.

The successful terrorist is always attacking, always escalating the character of his violence, but he must learn to regulate the escalation within prescribed bounds. At best each new tactic capable of raising the level of outrage and revulsion must be seen as a natural response to "the provocation of officials". At the very least, new tactics must be justified on grounds that the previous and more restrained efforts have not produced the desired effects.

The problem of justification is always a critical one, even within the terrorist movement itself, as Camus' magnificent play, *The Just Assassins*, so well illustrates. A few may become terrorists fully conscious of the enormities their decision implies. But many drift into terrorism gradually, prisoners of their own logic, adopting more extreme measures as each preceding one proves inadequate. When elections fail, one turns to demonstrations; when that seems useless, empty buildings are blown up; when that brings no results, kidnapping and finally murder seem logical. But even when the necessity to murder is accepted, it is difficult to rid ourselves of our compulsions to distinguish between offending officials, innocent bystanders, and those who sympathize with our aims but reject our means. The principle applies with even stronger force to the public at large. Each new tactic offends different sensibilities, but if the terrorist reveals how far he is prepared to go all at once, potential sympathizers will be appalled and the resistance immensely strengthened. The reaction to the recent strangulation of Minister Pierre Laporte is an obvious case in point.

The first phase of a terrorist campaign is the preparation period when the plotters are invisible to the public. They are drawing up plans, establishing organizations, gathering supplies, and creating bases. Experience suggests that in a city every terrorist unit requires at least three to four bases and that for each person actually engaged in acts of terror, seven to ten perform the vital information-gathering, gun-running, and base-maintenance functions.

To ward off the possibility of police penetration, terrorist organizations follow Nachaeyeff's recommendation of forming tiny, loosely tied cells, the organizer choosing longtime personal friends. The early Russian terrorists eagerly recruited women,

Nachaeyeff considering them the most important element of the movement, and women have played significant roles ever since. Some reasons are obvious. Terrorists depend *entirely* upon surprise, and because a woman generally draws less apprehension than a man she can surprise us more easily. A man with a briefcase is a more unusual and more easily remembered sight than a woman with a purse or shopping bag, but either may be transporting lethal materials. Policemen always seem more hesitant to search large numbers of women as thoroughly as they do men. Furthermore, at the beginning of a terrorist campaign, and perhaps afterwards, too, the police rely on males as undercover agents. Other less obvious reasons are relevant too. Terrorist manuals so often praise women that one might believe that the terrorists are convinced that once having made the commitment women seem less bothered by the frequent public taunt that terrorist attacks are cowardly or unmanly.

The terrorist fights a "poor man's war". Always short of cash and constantly in motion, his weapons must be inexpensive, small, light, and difficult to detect; whenever possible they should be items he can make or at least maintain himself. Excellent examples are fire bombs or bottled gasoline and lye bombs, made by injecting the acid into the metal ends of a light bulb.

In the second stage the terrorist makes himself known to the general public. When the terrorists may number only two or three dozen persons, when they are still untrained and untried, when they lack confidence in themselves, they must, if they want to continue to gain strength, have a few victories — victories which do not cost them casualties. So they attack the most defenseless targets, ones which apparently have no military or political value whatsoever — they plant fire bombs in office buildings, post offices, university libraries, and banks. No matter that the public regards these acts as infantile vandalism, criminal madness, or political lunacy. In the beginning what really matters is the training, experience, and confidence of the terrorist's organization. These exploits, he knows, will attract recruits, for they will be noticed by a special audience which did not know of his existence before, that small number in *every* population who perpetually dream of revolution or find it impossible to work through prescribed means. The terrorist signals them that a new phase of resistance has begun, shows how impotent government can be, and issues an invitation to join or imitate him. The longer the major portion of the public regards him as an infantile revolutionary, the more time he will have to solidify his organizational underpinnings.

The terrorist relies, as Nachaeyeff said he must, on the power of the propaganda of the deed, a power Lenin grossly underestimated partly because early terrorists did not know how to use it effectively. Modern communications multiply that power manyfold. Listen, for example, to Jerry Rubin's description of how his generation independently rediscovered the old Anarchist doctrine — — the exaggeration and enormous confusions involved should not obscure the truth contained here:

> You can't be a revolutionary today without a color television set — it's as important as a gun! . . .
> The first student demonstration flashed across the TV tubes . . . in 1964. That year the first generation being raised from birth on TV was 9, 10, and 11 years old. 'First chance I get,' they thought, 'I wanna do that too.'
> The first chance they got was when they got to junior high and high school five years later — 1969! And that was the year . . . [those] schools exploded. . . .
> Television proves the domino theory; one campus falls and they all fall. . . .
> TV transforms a demonstration, turning us into heroes. We take more chances when the press is there because we know that whatever happens will be known to the entire world within hours.
> Politicians get air time just by issuing statements. But ordinary people must take to the streets to get on television.
> Our power lies in our ability to strike fear in the enemy's heart so the more the media exaggerates, the better.

The first time fire or lye bombs explode, the fact makes headlines. As they are repeated again and again fewer people notice, and the campaign must be stepped up with more spectacular incidents. Robbing a bank or raiding an arms depot provides more publicity than setting off a bomb in a deserted office building, and it yields valuable funds or equipment as well to continue the struggle.

But, initially, publicity value is more important than the immediate material rewards. The terrorist must keep in mind which of several possible audiences he wants to impress. It is useful always, for example, to cultivate international opinion, which contains elements ready to aid some other country's rebels. While still an unknown guerrilla in the mountains, Castro effected a magnificent publicity coup by kidnapping a popular Argentine sports hero for several weeks, drawing the entire world's attention and much material and moral support to his movement. A few raids on banks and arms depots by the FLQ made foreigners everywhere (and perhaps most Canadians too) suddenly aware that Canada had an unresolved problem serious enough to foment difficulties between the French and Canadian governments. Similarly, after World War I, Irish attacks on British installations induced the U.S. to respond to the demands of Irish-Americans to exert pressures on the United Kingdom.

After his daring and cause are publicized and he has made government appear foolish and inept, the terrorist attempts to force government to act in ways to stir the strategic portions of the public potentially sympathetic to him. In contrast to his early predecessor who could think of nothing but assassinating prominent officials, the modern terrorist focuses on provoking persons most of us feel much more ambivalent about — such as the police. From his previous experiences as a demonstrator he has learned that they can be forced into areas where a great antagonism to their presence exists, such as the university, and where police often angrily respond to rioters in brutal, occasionally criminal ways. Soon students who call themselves "moderate" are saying that it is impossible to remain neutral between the "violence of the police and the militants". When students make the forces equivalent, and fail to note that when you kick someone he generally kicks back, the terrorists have succeeded in transforming ambivalence into favorable sentiment in a large, significant constituency, a fact which becomes even clearer when students refer to the "battle between pigs and militants". Their choice of terms indicates where their real sympathies lie. "When planning a demonstration," Jerry Rubin writes, "always include a role for the cops. Most people

CAMROSE LUTHERAN COLLEGE
LIBRARY

don't get excited until the cops come in. Nothing radicalizes like a cop. Cops are perfectly dressed for the role of the 'bad guy'."

Armed agents of the state serving in police capacities are obligated to use no more than the *minimum* force necessary to restrain illegal acts. Whether they will or not depends upon their training, sense of responsibility, emotional involvement, and the character of their provocation. Men may be so poorly trained that they will abandon responsibilities in the face of abusive tongues and "dirty" or homemade weapons. Witness the "police riot" of 1968 during the Democratic Convention in Chicago and the more recent Kent State Massacre. When the public imagines that all responsibilities for the events are fixed once the original provokers are identified, it strengthens the terrorist unwittingly. On the other hand, in Kenya where the Mau-Mau, in order to provoke superbly disciplined forces, made the deaths of their victims as lingering and disgusting as possible, British authorities pursued a wiser and juster policy of punishing the few officers who broke under the pressure.

As that extraordinary film, *The Battle of Algiers*, which is now a pictorial manual for terrorists, shows, a modern campaign early singles out policemen for indiscriminate assassination. In Cyprus, Algeria, Venezuela, and the United States, where some fifty officers have been murdered in the last year, the pattern has been the same. Many consequences flow from these attacks, and one scarcely noticed is extremely important. The police become consumed with the problem of self-protection; no officer travels alone any more, and police stations become heavily guarded. Fewer resources are available for their prime function, protection of the public, encouraging the normal criminal elements to become bolder and increasing distractions, dissatisfactions, fears, and hatred.

The relation between terrorist and criminal elements is not simply a matter of two different but coinciding interests. Recall that Nachaeyeff held the criminal to be the only true revolutionary and that Jerry Rubin hails Bonnie and Clyde as his generation's heroes. In France and Italy during the first terrorist wave at the turn of the century and in Venezuela more recently, men with long and vile criminal records suddenly declared themselves revolutionaries. One wonders how many juveniles have found it easier to become criminals if they can say they are serving justice.

Certainly the Black Panthers have turned the state's prisons into *their* recruiting centers. When we remember Marx and Lenin's contempt for the suggestion that ordinary criminals could contribute to the cause, the enormous difference between the classic revolutionary and the terrorist is driven home.

The attacks against those exercising police powers have more obvious consequences. The Irish terrorist Sean Casey said that if one murdered a few English soldiers, the army would goad all Ireland to revolt. To understand the force of his argument one must remember that the murder is less important than the unpredictable circumstances in which it occurs. A policeman who can never understand which situations are likely to be dangerous will become "trigger-happy" in all chance encounters with unknown members of the public. To reach for a cigarette during a conversation with a policeman may have disastrous consequences. If many terrorists are members of a particular social class, all individuals of that class may feel the burden of the policeman's anxiety, and inevitably their sympathy for the terrorist's cause will increase. The effect of terror always is to dissolve confidence in the conventions used to establish guilt and innocence.

The police have good reason to press for extraordinary powers. Should the government find itself unable to grant legitimate emergency powers, like curfew, the outlawing of particular organizations, etc., some policemen may take the law into their own hands, creating a disastrous, sometimes uncontrollable, situation. In America where it is still legal for the Black Panthers to collect arms, apprehensive police forces have launched brutal attacks which have created sympathies for the Panthers.

Information is the key to a successful campaign against terrorists. Fundamentally, the police have three principal sources of information — citizens who voluntarily report suspicious events, undercover agents, and the terrorists or terrorist sympathizers themselves. When police become deeply dependent upon the last two sources, the situation becomes most dangerous, and to a large extent this dependency is generated by an improper haste to secure information quickly. Undercover agents to establish their credit with the terrorists have often acted as provocateurs. Leaving aside the moral enormities involved, repeated actions of this sort undermine the government's credit. Equally important, the police in some countries have used terror or torture on suspects. In the long run more problems are created than solved. Most suspects are either innocent or do not have the information desired; when released they may become terrorists and/or the stories they tell will create more animosity towards the police and ultimately the government. In time the sensibilities of the public at large will be disturbed as the French paratroopers in Algeria and the British Black and Tans in Ireland found out.

In the last stage of the terrorist campaign, before the revolutionaries develop true military forces and later in conjunction with them, the terrorists must take the struggle out of the government's hands and place it into those of the major civilian protagonists. The first targets are people likely to support the government, and the object is to provoke them into senseless fury. Bombs explode in supermarkets, hospitals, nursery schools, and football stadiums — anywhere where large numbers may be concentrated or in any place where the defenseless are likely to be. In Algeria French settlers became so enraged that they formed vigilante committees to go on "Arab hunts", murdering every Arab they could find. Not surprisingly, the harassed police lacked vigilance in pursuing their obligation to stop them.

The second class of critical targets in this stage are those searching for a middle ground, the reformers who believe that if certain grievances the terrorist has been championing were attended to, his movement would dissipate. The terrorist himself realizes this possibility; and since his aim is revolution not the settlement of grievances, the reformers must be eliminated. There can be no middle ground — no degrees of attachment; you're either for the revolution or against it. "If you're not part of the solution you must be part of the problem." And if you are declared an enemy, the terrorist may feel that his cause is better served by murdering your child than you yourself. In this stage atrocities and mutilations are more frequent than ever before, and sometimes the terrorist goes too far. The tide finally turned against the Mau-Mau in Kenya when hundreds of Kikuyus were burned alive, pregnant women disemboweled, and children chopped to pieces.

A major purpose of the fourth stage is to force that great mass of ambivalents who desire amenities to realize that the state can no longer provide them, cannot even protect those who seek its services or comply with its law. To use the school, pay taxes, record a deed, get a marriage license, have a business dispute adjudicated, is to sign a death warrant which may be executed at any time against any person and in any brutal way. If you desire amenities, you *must* use terrorist facilities, facilities which necessarily operate in secrecy and darkness with all the attendant abuses. As more and more citizens say, "I, too, fear the terror more than anything else," the movement gets closer and closer towards its goal — to become the source of all political authority.

Terrorism whether successful or not always leaves bitter legacies. No one forgets atrocities. The decentralized character of the terrorist organization and the easy way in which new movements can form, means that the struggle always gets out of control. The FLN murdered eight times as many Algerians and at least as many terrorists and revolutionaries as they did Frenchmen! Ireland and Cyprus reveal similar pictures. Terrorism may divide a people so fundamentally that if a large portion does not leave, as was the case in the American colonies, Ireland, and Algeria, the hatred may persist indefinitely.

Only the Israeli terrorists avoided creating lasting divisions among their own people, that is if we except the effect of murders on the Arab element. The Israeli advantage was a peculiar circumstance, namely, the entire Jewish population really wanted independence, and terrorists could assault the British and Arabs alone. Even so the determination not to attack Jews was put to a severe test, for when Ben Gurion, the nation's leader, tried to suppress them and *allegedly* supplied several hundred names to the British authorities, many terrorists wanted to retaliate. But they did not, and as far as I know no comparable instance of terrorist restraint exists.

"In the land of the timid, the wild man rules"; if this is not the terrorist motto, it should be. Two hundred men and women aided by 1,300 sympathizers tore Algiers, a city of 700,000, apart for one year. But despite spectacular exploits the terrorist has *never* succeeded in provoking a massive uprising except in colonial territories, and even there he has failed much more often than he has succeeded.

Ireland illustrates the critical character of the colonial context well. The IRA gathered immense support when London ruled, but when the government was seated in Dublin, the IRA attempt to keep the revolution going became pathetic. In Latin America where conditions seem appropriate for revolution and where governments are often weak, fear-ridden, and inept, the terrorist has never yet succeeded.

Defeating the terrorist is partly a technical art requiring reliable information. Since the terrorist depends completely upon surprise, we can crush him easily if we know where he is or where he will be. The campaign, therefore, is *primarily* a task for policemen not soldiers, and it will take time for police measures to be effective. A government can afford to be patient, for in the long run the odds in its favor are overwhelming. To secure reliable information one must maintain proper relations with the public, and while in the short run it often seems sensible to fight terror with terror, a public accustomed to being governed according to law will ultimately turn on a government which forgets its primary charge.

The terrorist organization is peculiarly vulnerable because the tiny cell cannot protect its hideouts and bases once they are discovered. In the city, where the terrorist operates best, bases cannot be hidden indefinitely; chance encounters and informants will constantly reveal them. The terrorist must retreat to more favorable terrain for regrouping and recuperation — that is, he must go to the countryside; that in turn means that he must have guerrilla support. The only modern exception is Cyprus, where for two years before he struck, Grivas utilized the extraordinary rocky terrain to prepare an elaborate series of hideouts and arms caches in the island's innumerable caves. The original Society of Assassins was an exception, too; the movement remained invulnerable for more than two and a half centuries because no Moslem army was strong enough to storm its mountain base until the great warrior Tamerlane came on the scene.

Despite capacities to wreak much destruction, without guerrilla-defended bases the modern terrorist cannot succeed. And since the guerrillas themselves need one last sanctuary beyond the jurisdiction of the existing government, a neighboring power at least must be willing to cast a blind eye on movements across its borders.

Less easy to define are the internal political conditions for terrorist activity, and time precludes me from making more than one or two comments. If the grievances the terrorist is championing can be satisfied, it makes sense to do so. But even when the will and possibility exist, the practical difficulties are immense. To yield to terror is to deliver an open invitation to other groups to use terror themselves. Moreover, by settling grievances we are at best simply cutting the terrorist's potential support, not eliminating the terrorist himself, who will be the first to tell us that he wants "everything right now". The police, therefore, must finish the job.

Terrorism is the product of an ambivalent society, as Nachaeyeff realized, where men are uncertain about their priorities and vulnerable to the possessed who know how to exploit their confusions dramatically. But ambivalence alone is not sufficient. The group which the terrorist hopes ultimately to lead must be large, concentrated, and have immense underlying hostility to the dominant social element. It must be clearly differentiated by visible characteristics, such as dress, class, language, race, or culture so that massive indiscriminate retaliation attacks can be launched by those who are the initial victims of terror. So far this condition has only been fulfilled in colonial territories, where the dominant group feels guilty about its superiority and the leaders of the subordinate groups have the uneasy feeling that they have betrayed their people and shamed themselves by participating in and enjoying the personal benefits of the constitutional process.

Future terrorists may demonstrate that the ambivalent society is not confined to colonial situations. Even if they cannot, terrorism has been successful enough to inspire fresh attempts again and again in other countries. All of us will see a lot more terrorist activity before we see less.

The fathers have eaten sour grapes and the children's teeth are set on edge.
Ezekiel.

Many observers compared Europe's discontents in 1968 with its revolutionary upsurges in 1848. Juxtaposing these two points in American history yields even more startling parallels.[1] In some respects the issues raised are identical; even the very scene today looks like a repeat performance.

In 1848 the Mexican War deeply divided America. The opposition, including the young Congressman Abraham Lincoln, accused the President of deceitfully manipulating Congress into declaring an unwanted, unjust war. So extraordinary did the credibility question seem, so powerful were the passions evoked, that one scholar much later, from the vantage of the more placid Eisenhower administration, characterized the situation as one beyond the range of the modern American's political imagination.

> Today it is almost inconceivable that we should be involved in a foreign war in which the President could be denounced as the aggressor and a foreign enemy could be described as the victim by leading members of the opposition. Lincoln's denunciation of [President] Polk in the House came very close to what a later and an earlier age would call treason or at least criminal disloyalty.[2]

Then as now the war was inseparable from the nation's racial

1. I am indebted to my colleague Leo Snowiss for suggesting the possibility of a fruitful comparison of 1848 and 1968.
2. H. V. Jaffa, *Crisis of the House Divided* (New York, 1959), p. 67. Lincoln himself was denounced in similar terms when he became President. Although Lyndon Johnson discomforted critics by comparing himself to Lincoln during the Civil War, neither he nor they seemed to grasp the irony of Lincoln's fate.

predicament. The opposition of '48 insisted that the war was undertaken to spread slave territory; today most believe that the unintended consequence of Vietnam is a massive diversion of energies from the prime domestic question — justice for the black man. Earlier, impatience with the existing constitutional procedures stimulated first a doctrine of civil disobedience, vividly expressed by Anarchists like Thoreau, and then a fascination with violent direct action as represented by Abolitionists like John Brown. Recently the pattern has been repeated again.

In both periods, a President decided not to run for a second term. Earlier, the majority coalition forged by Jackson collapsed; nowadays, the Roosevelt coalition is in shambles. When the Mexican War ended, domestic opponents became *more* rather than *less* inflexible; and there are good reasons to think that the same thing will happen again.

These parallels are not simply striking sets of coincidences. Every system has it own perennial moral questions; in raising one, impulses are generated to raise the others again.[3] Constitutions, moreover, channel outrage in specific directions. In America indignation concerning war immediately involves the President, so comprehensive is his responsibility for foreign policy and for military movements. When the black question is re-examined, the party arrangements are threatened, because ever since the Civil War regional and national alliances have been composed in the light of certain assumptions concerning the black man's place in the system.

What then distinguishes 1968 from 1848? Most contemporaries would say that we have a "generation gap" while they did not. Yet Lincoln's speeches suggest that his period had this problem, too. In 1838, he interpreted the growing propensity to mob violence throughout all portions of America to signify that his generation was in spiritual revolt against its fathers, who had established the constitution. The result could be catastrophic:

> That our government should have been maintained
> in its original form from its establishment until now,

3. The movement for "female emancipation" in America began in the 1840s, and during the present discontents the issue has been revived in the Women's Liberation Front and similar groups.

is not much to be wondered at. It had many props to support its establishment through that period which now are decayed, and crumbled away. Through that period it was felt by all to be an undecided experiment; now it is understood to be a successful one. Then, all that sought celebrity and fame and distinction, expected to find them in the success of that experiment. Their all was staked upon it; their destiny was inseparably linked with it. Their ambition aspired to display before an admiring world, a practical demonstration of the truth of a proposition, which had hitherto been considered, at best no better, than problematical; namely the capability of a people to govern themselves. If they succeeded they were to be immortalized. . . . If they failed, they were to be called knaves and fools and fanatics. . . . They succeeded. . . . [T]he game is caught; and I believe it is true, that with the catching, end the pleasures of the chase. This field of glory is harvested, and the crop is already appropriated. But new reapers will arise and they, too, will seek a field. . . . The question then is can [their ruling passion] be gratified in supporting and maintaining an edifice erected by others. Most certainly it cannot. . . . Towering genius disdains a beaten path. It seeks no distinction in adding story to story, upon the monuments of fame erected to the memory of others. It denies that it is glory enough to serve under any chief. It scorns to tread in the footsteps of any predecessor, however illustrious. *It thirsts and burns for distinction; and if possible, it will have it, whether at the expense of empancipating slaves or enslaving freemen* [my emphasis].

I

There are differences between the rivalry of generations in 1848 and 1968. Earlier the conflict involved a "competition" between the dead and the living who were unable to confront each other directly. There was no recognizable political distinction between young and old men for the young lacked a belief in their own unity. As society's most passionate elements, the young became militants within existing social groupings, and the ensuing violence was largely *between* youths.

"Youth" today is self-conscious and the battle is joined directly with the old. The extraordinary expansion of the universities has given youth a predominant occupation and provided spawning grounds for his political energies. Visualize the difference between 1848 and 1968 in Marxist categories: the young men of the 19th century, like Marx's peasant, were too dispersed to see themselves as members of a class, but the geography of the university, like that of the factory before it, has wrought a fundamental change.

For several decades, the development of youth as a class was becoming visible before that unity was expressed in political terms. After World War II the affluence of suburban life gave young men time and money. They constituted a special *market,* a unique sub-culture, and their needs were stimulated and communicated by mass media and satisfied by mass production. The sense of common identity grew stronger and more definite in time, embracing wider and wider ranges of activities.

Mass luxury markets are created by advertisers, so the New Left would have us believe. If the dogma is true, a delicious neo-Marxist dialectical irony could be in process. For though youth is only an "artificial" class fashioned by the hated hucksters, still it, like all real dialectical classes, will finally destroy its creator. Marx argued that the virility of new classes, the reason for their victory, lay in their productive capacities. The weaknesses of the old classes, and the cause for their ultimate extinction, derives from their parasitic condition. Modern youth, however, unlike the bourgeoisie, has never produced, has always been simply a consumer or a parasite. And youth *knows* himself to be a parasite!

A sense of his own shame gives fuel to the youth's desperation. It thwarts his search for worthy allies. Workers, especially younger ones, openly flaunt their contempt. The black man, the prime object of the youth's advances, rubs salt into open wounds, asking the student radical how one who has never worked, never suffered, and never will suffer because his parents are middle class, can ever be reliable. The need to demonstrate that he is not a parasite, that he's not playing at a game which involves no permanent risks, conditions the youth's tactics. When the Students for a Democratic Society crumbled in June 1969, the principal factions taunted each other with cries of "comfortable revolutionary" and "parasite". All factions felt compelled to leave the university, their natural constituency and sanctuary, to prove themselves in the society at large. The Weathermen, the most belligerent element, openly compared themselves to the middle-class student revolutionaries of late 19th-century Russia "going back to the peasants and terrorism".

As Lincoln noted, the conflict between generations always has deep unconscious roots, and the frantic behavior of our youth has, as one might expect, provided American psychiatrists with delightful possibilities. Bruno Bettelheim has written one of the more sensible accounts, "Obsolete Youth: Towards a Psychograph of Adolescent Rebellion";[4] it has been widely discussed in the universities, although now that Vice-President Agnew has endorsed the argument in a prepared speech on 10 December 1969, one wonders how seriously academics will continue to treat it.

Bettelheim believes that the issues youth addresses itself to are not those which really concern them, and that the solution to present difficulties presupposes that Americans realize that they "prolong adolescence long beyond that which any other period in history thought desirable". In adolescence, Bettelheim notes, the search for identity culminates in excruciating agony and stimulates the most violent aggressive impulses, which are directed alternatively against society and against oneself. The adolescent cannot wait to become a man, to prove that he has the relevant knowledge and firmness. A century ago, most young men assumed a productive role earlier. But society no longer automatically provides means for establishing their worth; for, Bettelheim notes, we have become so wealthy that the time young men must provide for themselves can be postponed. We keep them in school too long and compound natural frustrations by the sense of dependency that an education paid for by someone else always fosters. "Since they feel themselves to be parasites . . . they come to hate a world which gives them such a feeling."

Today youth is dominated by hate, not a desire for a better world. His fascination with violence, contempt for reason, craving for destruction and revenge, passionate effort to use political causes to create personal significance — all these things and many more

4. *Encounter,* September 1969, pp. 29-42.

stem from his own suspicion that he lacks real worth. Bettelheim's simple solution, identical to the one the philosopher William James propounded in "The Moral Equivalent of War" nearly sixty years ago, is a compulsory "youth service programme for a few years' duration in which young people could work on socially relevant projects while earning pay and getting higher professional training as they do".

Although much in Bettelheim's discussion is worth commending, the moral and political issues youth raises cannot be explained away by reference to *their* psychic disorders and *our* badly contrived institutions. When Bettelheim uses this formula alone to explain why students object so violently to the Vietnam War, even readers most sympathetic to his diagnosis will wince. The Government, he says, has stupidly allowed students special exemption from the draft, thus arousing massive guilt feelings. "Because if I am exempt from serving in Vietnam while others are not I can only live in peace with myself by believing it an amoral war. (As if there ever was a moral war!)" (Now that Americans have introduced a lottery in the conscription process, Bettelheim's thesis will be put to the test!)

But let us lay the various moral and political questions aside in order to grapple with Bettelheim on his own ground. Profoundly disturbed children usually have uneasy, insecure parents; and if a real source of the youth's problems are his parents, can his discontent be properly treated by legislative enactments alone?

Plato argued that the relationship of generations is the key concept in any treatment of political change. The contradictions and ambivalences of the father come to light in the son, who forms a different uneasy equilibrium which subsequently dissolves in the disorders of his progeny. The concept is simple and well-known, pregnant with immense possibilities and subtle elaborations. Yet no American social scientist seems to have grasped the idea, for although enormous energies have been spent studying the psychic disturbances of youth, the parents have remained ignored and are, presumably, uninteresting subjects.

Bettelheim, it is true, does see the trace of another trail or two, as he hurries after bigger game. As a psychiatrist he finds the enormous change in child-rearing patterns since World War II disturbing. We have been spoiling our children, being "unwilling to risk displeasure from the child by imposing controls" — a tendency which has been strengthened by a vulgar misinterpretation of Freud's teaching to suggest that repression is wrong. Lacking a true justification for punishment, we coerce and yield erratically, as *our* convenience, not the need of the child, dictates. The child learns that punishment is inconsistent and vindictive, and intuitively senses our guilt and indecision. Unwittingly we teach him that we can be bullied, and he goes through life thinking that everyone else can be pushed around, too.

A father who cannot discipline his son is obviously uncertain of his own right to rule. He cannot respect his own standards. A crucial question is what does he really think of himself? Bettelheim, unfortunately, does not treat the question; in fact he makes no effort to demonstrate his belief that insecure, permissive parents do produce student revolutionaries. Although laymen have always been quick to relate student discontent to the failure of parents, academics, for reasons interesting to speculate about, have generally ignored the suggestion. The evidence of Samuel Lubell's essay, "That 'Generation Gap'", although collected for different purposes, however, does indicate that youths who resist student radicalism or use of drugs mostly come from strictly run homes.[5]

II

Why has the father lost confidence in himself?[6] One important reason, generally overlooked, is that we no longer believe that age gives a man seasoning and perspective. In societies where age was respected, the presumption had to be that as one grew older, one gained more experience, and hence wisdom, to handle the same recurring problems. Now the very word wisdom sticks in our throats, especially and paradoxically, it should be added, in the

5. *The Public Interest*, Autumn, 1968, pp. 52-60.
6. I am concentrating on the father but the mother is obviously crucial. The psychiatrist, Kenneth Keniston, who generally approves of student radicals, argues that they come from homes where the female is dominant and the male submissive. (Kenneth Keniston, *The Young Radicals*, Harcourt, Brace and World, New York, 1968.)

universities. Even if we understood what it could possibly have meant once, we would be too embarrassed to use it now. What place is there for wisdom when social scientists, journalists, and politicians day after day declare every issue revolutionary, when we are told that the past only teaches us that we are different, when we say that all forms of "skills" and knowledge will be soon antiquated, when the very term "modern" suggests something better and something which has never happened before!

Quite obviously there is some truth in the picture Americans paint of themselves, but the monstrous distortions involved are passed over quickly especially in the universities, where the lust for novelty becomes almost unbearable. Whatever their real intention, the parents and the universities have declared themselves irrelevant, suggested that youth experiences something we cannot comprehend, and indicated our envy for their good fortune. Can we blame youth for calling us hypocrites when we will not or cannot yield our official status?

These comments may shed light on the contribution of the "educated" parents and the universities to the youth's agony; they do not illuminate the relation between the *political* aspirations of the two generations. Every study shows that the overwhelming number of leading student revolutionaries come from liberal or left-wing homes. Bettelheim explains that the "son has a desperate wish to do better than the parents, especially where the parent has become weak in his beliefs". The young, hence, do accept the values of their parents, but they detect ambivalence and differences between private talk and public behavior, and they aim to eliminate inconsistencies. The real question, the one everyone ignores, is what happened to the older generation's search for political identity?

Our formative political experiences were depression, war, and post-war recovery. The depression made many hate the community while simultaneously stimulating splendid hopes that they could create a brighter better one to replace it. Contrary to expectation, war revitalized the constitution. Pearl Harbor gave us an indisputably just cause, being the first war in American history to raise no moral doubts, and the victory produced an immense fund of credit which carried us through the post-war period. Unemployment, the most visible evil of the Thirties, disappeared. Our recovery seemed miraculous, a product of circumstance rather than conscious effort.

Some critics obviously had a genuine change of heart and recognized that they had been blind to the constitution's virtues and potentialities. But many were stilled because the constitution's success dazzled them, because there were no alternatives, because they accepted what they *said* they would always despise or reject — money and status — or because they felt too weary or vulnerable to continue the fight. Such men cannot be truly reconciled; the feeling that they have been unworthy gnaws at their souls, distorting their thoughts, language, and deeds.

Note the reaction of one old reformer, now a prominent educator and consultant, to the demands of the young:

> My generation accepted the precepts of its parents. . . . The new generation rejects them. We were wrong and the new generation is right. Our precepts were good but still the new generation is right. They are right because preceptorial is as preceptorial does. We were — and, of course, are — pious frauds. They are impious Abelards . . . .
>
> It was an unjust America of course. Blacks were Negroes, Negroes were niggers and niggers were ineducable. . . . Jews knew their place and did not take forcible possession of the boardroom. The revolution is long overdue — the revolution which Jeremiah and Jefferson invoked when they said that God's justice would not sleep forever. The evils that were containable under kings are no longer containable under politicians. [Our world] . . . is not susceptible of reform. It calls for revolution . . . .
>
> I am one of the elders of whom I speak. The young terrify me. They terrify me because I have mine, which I got by the exercise of good precepts I learned from my parents plus being white and landing on my feet every time I fell on my face.[7]

What can the young learn from one who declares *himself* a "pious fraud", states that the position *he* occupies is unrelated to his merit, and implies that he might be a coward? An answer is contained in Dostoyevsky's *The Possessed*, a novel much in vogue

7. Professor Milton Mayer, "Children's Crusade: A Search for Light", *Los Angeles Times*, 16 November 1969.

among our youth, for there, too, the older or liberal generation feels that it has betrayed its dreams and wallows in self-contempt. Creatures of the establishment, they "relieve" their guilt by spiteful talk about everyone and everything around them, and are haunted by a passage from Revelation: "I know thy work, that thou art neither cold nor hot: I would thou wert cold or hot. So then because thou art lukewarm . . . I will spew thee out of my mouth."

Sour grapes did set the child's teeth on edge. The son became a nihilist whose creed was sincerity. Acting out his father's fantasies he stormed the walls of Jericho with trumpet blasts. A single "moral" deed would dissolve a corrupt world, or, at least, he reckoned that in the country of the timid the bold always triumph.

The hatred of our youth appalls us because it results in senseless destructive acts. But the hatred of our "enlightened" middle-aged, manifested in constant, cheap, and captious talk, scarcely draws our attention. When egalitarianism was not taken for granted, men did probe the unconscious drives behind the liberal's rhetoric. Nietzsche, Dostoyevsky, and Sorel insisted that the liberal's idealization of the weak really masked a desire to wreak vengeance on the strong for his own inadequacies. They only caught a small portion of our subconscious but they did see an essential part, one which in different circumstances, when apprehension of immediate consequences wanes, becomes the dominant passion. The logic of *The Possessed* is that the distance between the desire to inflict or receive pain and an intense delight in doing so is only one generation.

The young really do not know what they want, we complain, but they could easily throw the complaint back in our faces if they weren't so busy exploiting our confusion. So often does the elder generation abandon ordinary standards of *truth* when confronted by moral dilemmas that the "guilt-ridden liberal" has become a great unanalysed truism of American politics in the past decade.

As one might expect the liberal's shame is most clearly revealed when the black question, American's perennial moral predicament, is discussed. In 1967 justice for the black meant indifference to the color of a man's skin. Integration or equal rights for *individuals* was the liberal ideal, an ideal consistent with the magnificent traditions of liberal thought. Nowadays, justice for the black means giving him special privileges and rights justified by the fact that he belongs to a separate *community* defined by skin color. Of course deeper reflection on the meaning of justice may lead one to believe that it was right to alter our basic assumption, but this enormous shift took place in two years without much discussion or soul-searching. Did we believe segregation bad when advocated by southern whites and good when it became the policy of the most militant blacks? Ironically, most blacks do not want segregation, and our sentimentalism may in effect make their lot even more cruel, or so Bayard Rustin, whose credentials as a devoted black leader are beyond question, tells us:

> It is not the *lumpen-proletariat*, the Negro working classes, the Negro working poor, who are proclaiming: 'We want Negro principals, we want Negro supervisors, we want Negro teachers in our schools.' It is the educated Negroes. . . . Being blocked from moving up, [they] become not only interested in Negro children, but in getting those teaching jobs, supervisory jobs, and principal jobs for [their] own economic interest.[8]

The belated and massive rush of the universities, those great well-springs of American liberalism, to deal with the black question demonstrates the same shameful unwillingness to apply ordinary standards of argument and justice. Many have adopted a quota system virtually guaranteeing that the number of black students will be equal to the proportion of black citizens; some academics use double standards of grading; these changes and others as serious are taking place without public consideration of the implications for other minorities, for the nation as a whole, or for the university.

We do not even question the implications for the blacks themselves. Liberals confide that the black man will never have pride and self-confidence until his community has its share of professional men, that this crash program is a temporary arrange-

8. "Towards Integration as a Goal", *Separatism or Integration: Which Way for America* (A. Phillip Randolph Education Fund, 1968), p. 18. The parallel with our attitudes towards the underdeveloped world is striking. The liberal's "benevolence" made him tolerate dictatorships everywhere as long as dictators used the right slogans.

ment, and that in time blacks will compete with whites as equals. But currently what happens to the pride of the black who knows he has a second-class degree, what happens to his patient or client, and what happens if the purposes of the programs are corrupted? Nobody asks, for who can live with the charge of "racism"?

Does the liberal's guilt prevent him from being truly responsible to the black, from treating him as a man capable of foolish as well as wise actions? In the autumn of 1969 I attended a faculty assembly which vigorously applauded black students who illustrated the meaning of academic freedom to us by quoting extensive passages from the writings of Nkrumah! And yet we continue to lament that our youth is contemptuous.

III

One of the more interesting features of modern youth is his taste for Civil War clothing and hair styles. It is almost as though he is searching for the attire appropriate to relive the most profound emotional upheaval in American history. The wild talk about guerrilla war among the student radicals and the historical parallels to the issues raised give this interpretation superficial plausibility.

But the awesome epic of 19th-century America will not be repeated. Youth is too parasitic, and his status too transitory for him to create more than a few sporadic and weak terrorist movements. In this respect it would pay us all to look at the experience of 19th-century Russia again, where student fury antagonized the peasants and induced the Tsars to halt projected reforms.

In the 1950s when Joseph McCarthy dominated the American scene, apologists used to infuriate liberals by noting that good ends were being accomplished by improper means. Today many liberals use identical arguments to justify student excesses. Youth they say has already improved the moral quality of American politics by compelling a re-examination of one war and calling attention to the black man's plight. Both points are testaments to the liberal's extraordinary indifference to our historical experiences. No student protested against the Korean War but when casualties mounted, the discontent of *voters* unseated a President and his party and forced withdrawal before a peace was concluded. In the more recent case, it is certainly conceivable that student violence over the Vietnam War actually intensified determination to hold on longer, and it did alienate traditional isolationist or anti-war sentiment in the country.

The young radical and middle-aged liberal fervently believe that the end of the Vietnam War will release sufficient energies to solve finally the black question — a question which, in one form or another, has been present ever since the colonial period. Let us hope they are right. Unfortunately, there are good reasons to think that the end of the war will make the situation worse. The blood shed by the black for his country will no longer be irresistible emotional "proof" of the justice of his demands; the need to end the war will no longer exist as a compelling reason to yield to domestic pressures; the costly irresponsible sentimentalism of liberal approaches will become more obvious; and, the worst tragedy of all, the black militant may discover that the rhetoric of segregation has made him more vulnerable than he ever thought possible.

The rancor and irresolution of the middle-aged have magnified America's difficulties immensely, while sapping the strength of our children to cope when they finally inherit our positions. How sour then will the grapes taste! What sort of children can *they* possibly produce?

APPENDIX: NACHAEYEFF'S "REVOLUTIONARY CATECHISM"

The Duties of the Revolutionary toward Himself

1. The revolutionary is a dedicated man. He has no personal inclinations, no business affairs, no emotions, no attachments, no property, and no name. Everything in him is subordinated towards a single exclusive attachment, a single thought, and a single passion — the revolution.

2. In the very depths of his being, not only in words but also in deeds, he has torn himself away from the bonds which tie him to the social order and to the cultivated world, with all its laws, moralities, and customs and with all its generally accepted conventions. He is their implacable enemy, and if he continues to live with them it is only in order to destroy them more quickly.

3. The revolutionary despises all dogmas and refuses to accept the mundane sciences, leaving them for future generations. He knows only one science: the science of destruction. For this reason, and only for this reason, he will study mechanics, physics, chemistry, and perhaps medicine. But all day and night he studies the living science of peoples, their characteristics and circumstances, and all the phenomena of the present social order. The object is the same: the prompt destruction of this filthy order.

4. The revolutionary despises public opinion. He despises and hates the existing social order in all its manifestations. For him, morality is everything which contributes to the triumph of the revolution. Immoral and criminal is everything that stands in his way.

5. The revolutionary is a dedicated man, merciless toward the state and altogether merciless toward the educated classes; and he can expect no mercy from them. Between him and them there exists, declared or concealed, a continual and irreconcilable war "for life or for death". He must accustom himself to enduring torture.

6. Tyrannical toward himself, he must be tyrannical toward others. All the soft and tender affections arising from kinship, friendship, and love, all gratitude and even all honor must be obliterated, and in their place there must be the cold and single-minded passion for the work of revolution. For him there exists only one pleasure, one consolation, one reward, one satisfaction — the success of the revolution. Night and day he must have but one thought, one aim — merciless destruction. Aiming cold-bloodedly and indefatigably toward this end, he must be ready to destroy himself and destroy with his own hands everyone who stands in his way.

7. The nature of the true revolutionary excludes all romanticism, all sensitivity, all exaltations and enthusiasms. He must also exclude private vendettas and personal hatred. The revolutionary passion, practised at every moment of the day until it becomes a habit, is to be employed with cold calculation. At all times and in all places the revolutionary must refuse to allow himself to be guided by his personal impulses, but only by the total submergence of himself in the revolution.

Relationship of the Revolutionary toward the Revolutionary Comrades

8. The revolutionary can have no friendly feeling to anyone unless, like him, the other is dedicated to revolutionary affairs. His degree of friendship, devotion, and obligation towards a comrade must be determined only by the degree of the comrade's usefulness in the practical work of complete and destructive revolution.

9. It is superfluous to speak of solidarity among revolutionaries. The whole strength of the revolutionary work lies in this. Comrades who possess the same revolutionary passion should, as much as possible, deliberate all important matters together

and come to unanimous conclusions. But the revolutionary, in accomplishing whatever plan is finally decided upon, must rely altogether on himself. The contract of revolutionary destruction demands that no comrades should come running up with advice and assistance if this detracts from the success of the plan.

10. Each comrade should have under him several revolutionaries of the second or third rank, i.e., comrades who are not completely dedicated. These should be regarded as portions of a common fund of revolutionary capital, to be expended as he thinks fit. He should expend them as economically as possible, always attempting to derive the utmost use from them. He should regard himself as capital consecrated to the triumph of the revolution; and he must not be regarded as expendable without the entire agreement of the fully initiated comrades.

11. When a comrade is caught in a dangerous extremity and the question arises whether he should be rescued or not rescued, the revolutionary must make his decision without recourse to personal feelings, but only in terms of the eventual success of the revolution. Therefore, it is necessary to balance carefully the usefulness of the comrade in so far as it is a question of revolutionary strength, and the most careful consideration should be made to decide whether he is worth rescuing.

Relationship of the Revolutionary toward Society

12. Whether a new member, after giving proof of loyalty by word and deed, should be accepted is a matter to be decided only by unanimous agreement.

13. The revolutionary enters the world of the state, of the classes and of so-called culture, and he lives in this world only because he has faith in its speedy and total destruction. He is not a revolutionary if he feels any sympathy for this world. He must not hesitate to destroy any position, any place, or any man in this world — all must be equally detested by him. All the worse for him if he has parents, friends, and loved ones; he is no longer a revolutionary if they can stay his hand.

14. Aiming at implacable destruction the revolutionary can, and sometimes must, live within society while pretending to be

other than what he is. A revolutionary must penetrate everywhere, among the lowest and the middle classes and in the houses of commerce, in the churches, in the palaces of the aristocracy. He must know the world of the bureaucrats and of the military and of literature, and he must enter into the Third Division and even into the Winter Palace.

15. All the members of this filthy society can be split up into several categories: the first category comprises those to be condemned to death without delay. The comrades should compile a list of those to be condemned, weighing the relative gravity of their crimes against their value to the revolution; and the executions should be carried out according to the prepared order.

16. In the preparation of these lists and in placing the condemned according to the prepared order, no private sense of outrage should be considered, nor is it necessary to pay attention to the hatred provoked by these people among the comrades or the people. But hatred and the sense of outrage must to some extent be made use of, because these things help to incite rebellion among the people. It is necessary to be guided only by the relative usefulness of these executions for the sake of the revolution. Above all, those who are especially inimical to the revolutionary organization must be destroyed; their violent and sudden deaths will produce the utmost panic in the government, it will shake the foundations of government and deprive it of the services of its most intelligent and energetic agents.

17. The second group consists of those to whom we concede life provisionally in order that their bestial behavior shall drive the people to inevitable revolt.

18. The third category consists of a multitude of personages or animals distinguished neither for intelligence nor for energy: those who enjoy wealth, connections, influence, and power. These must be exploited in every possible way; they must be implicated and confused; as far as possible their dirty secrets should be found out, so that we can make them our slaves. Their power, influence, and connections, their riches and energy, will form an inexhaustible treasure and a precious help in our various undertakings.

19. The fourth category is composed of ambitious people and liberals of various shades. We shall pretend we are following their ideas and give them cause to think we are blindly conspiring with them, while in fact we take them under our own control. We shall root out all their secrets and compromise them to the uttermost, so that there will be no way out for them and they can be used to create disorder in the state.

20. The fifth category consists of doctrinaires, conspirators, revolutionaries: all idle word-spillers who orate before meetings or in front of a piece of paper. They must be constantly driven forward to make violent declarations carefully arranged to agree with our purpose. The majority of these will leave nothing behind but a vast ruin; from a few of them we shall attain real revolutionary gains.

21. The sixth category is especially important: women. They should be divided into three chief divisions. First: those frivolous, thoughtless, and vapid women, whom we shall use as we use the third and fourth category of men. Second: women who are ardent, gifted, and devoted, but do not belong to us because they have not yet achieved a passionless and austere revolutionary understanding: these must be used like the men of the fifth category. Finally, there are the women who are completely on our side, i.e., those who are wholly dedicated and who have accepted our program in its entirety. We should regard these women as the most valuable of our treasures; without their help it would be impossible to succeed.

The Duties of our Society toward the People

22. The aims of our Society are none other than the entire emancipation and happiness of the people, i.e., the common laborers. Convinced that their emancipation and the achievement of this happiness is brought about only by means of an all-destroying popular revolt, we shall see that society will employ all its power, all its resources, towards increasing and intensifying the calamities and evils until their patience is exhausted and they will break out in a *levée-en-masse*.

23. By a popular revolution, the Society does not mean a revolution tailored according to the classic western model, a pattern

which is fundamentally restrained by the existence of property and the traditional social orders of so-called civilization and morality. Until now, such a civilization has cast down one political form only to substitute another, thereby attempting to bring about a so-called revolutionary state. The only salutory form of revolution is one which destroys the entire state to the roots and exterminates all imperial traditions, the whole social order, and all the existing classes in Russia.

24. With this end in view the Society refuses to impose any new organization from above. Any future organization will doubtless work its way through the movement and life of the people: but this is a matter for future generations to decide. Our task is terrible, total, universal, and merciless destruction. (. . . *strashnoe, polnoe, povsemestnoe i bezposhchadnoe razrusheniye.*)

25. Therefore, in drawing closer to the people, we must above all unite with those elements of popular life which, from the very beginning of the imperial power of Muscovy, have never ceased to protest, not only in words but in deeds, against everything directly or indirectly connected with the State: against the nobility, against the bureaucracy, against the priests, against business, and against the tight fist of the extortioner. We must unite with the adventurous tribes of brigands, who are the only true revolutionaries of Russia.

26. To knit the people into a single force which is wholly destructive and wholly invincible — such is our organization, our conspiracy, and our task.

BIBLIOGRAPHY

BOOKS

Arendt, Hannah. *The Origins of Totalitarianism,* rev. ed. New York: 1968.

Avineri, Shlomo. *The Social and Political Thought of Karl Marx,* London: 1968.

Avrich, Paul. *The Russian Anarchists,* Princeton: 1967.

Bebel, August. *Assassinations and Socialism,* New York: 1898.

Beck, F. and W. Godin. (pseuds.) *Russian Purge and the Extraction of Confession,* New York: 1951.

Black, J. B. *The Reign of Elizabeth,* Oxford: 1937.

Bornstein, Joseph. *The Politics of Murder,* New York: 1958.

Burckhardt, J. C. *The Civilization of the Renaissance in Italy,* London: 1937.

Byas, Hugh. *Government By Assassination,* London: 1943.

Camus, Albert. *Caligula and Three Other Plays,* New York: 1958.

Camus, Albert. *The Rebel,* New York: 1954.

Conquest, Robert. *The Great Terror,* New York: 1968.

Dallin, Alexander and G. Breslauer. *Political Terror in Communist Systems,* Stanford: 1970.

Dawson, Henry B. *The Sons of Liberty in New York,* New York: 1859.

DeWar, Hugo. *Assassins at Large,* New York: 1950.

Dostoyevsky, Fyodor. *The Possessed,* New York: 1931.

Fanon, Frantz. *The Wretched of the Earth,* London: 1969.

Figner, Vera. *Memoirs of a Revolutionist,* New York: 1927.

Gaucher, Roland. *The Terrorists,* London: 1968.

Goodspeed, D. J. *The Conspirators,* New York: 1962.

Gribble, Leonard. *Hands of Terror,* London: 1950.

Havens, Murray *et al. The Politics of Assassination,* New York: 1970.

Henissart, Paul. *Wolves in the City,* New York: 1970.

Hodgson, Marshall. *The Order of Assassins,* Gravenhage: 1955.

Hunter, Robert. *Violence and the Labor Movement,* New York: 1970.

Hyams, Edward. *Killing No Murder,* London: 1969.

Jacobs, Harold, ed. *The Weathermen,* New York: 1970.

Jaszi, Oscar and J. Lewis. *Against the Tyrant,* Glencoe: 1967.

Joll, James. *The Anarchists,* London: 1964.

Kedward, Roderick. *The Anarchists,* London: 1971.

Kirkham, James *et al. Assassination and Political Violence,* Washington: 1969.

Koestler, Arthur. *Darkness at Noon,* New York: 1961.

Lenin, Vladimir. *What Is To Be Done?* New York: 1929.

Lewis, Bernard. *The Assassins,* London: 1967.

London, Jack. *The Assassination Bureau Ltd.,* New York: 1963.

Machiavelli, Niccolo. *The Discourses,* New Haven: 1950. 2 vols.

Maine, Sir Henry. *Popular Government,* New York: 1886.

Merleau-Ponty, Maurice. *Humanism and Terror,* Boston: 1967.

Mommson, Theodor. *History of Rome,* London: 1929. 4 vols.

Montesquieu, Baron de. *Spirit of the Laws,* New York: 1900. 2 vols.

Moore, Barrington. *Terror and Progress — USSR,* Cambridge, Mass.: 1954.

Neumann, Sigmund. *Permanent Revolution,* 2nd ed., New York: 1965.

Pascal, Blaise. *The Provincial Letters*, London: 1896.

Payne, P. S. Robert. *Zero*, New York: 1950.

Postgate, Raymond. *How to Make a Revolution*, New York: 1938.

Powers, Thomas. *Diana: The Making of a Terrorist*, New York: 1971.

Randel, W. P. *The K.K.K.*, London: 1965.

Rauschning, Hermann. *Revolution of Nihilism*, New York: 1940.

Rubin, Jerry. *Do It*, New York: 1970.

Storry, Richard. *The Double Patriots*, Boston: 1957.

Symonds, J. A. *The Renaissance in Italy: Age of the Despots*, London: 1875.

Thomas, Aquinas, St. *On the Governance of Rulers*, Toronto: 1935.

Thomas, More, St. *Utopia*, London: 1887.

Walter, Eugene V. *Terror and Resistance*, New York: 1969.

Woodcock, George. *Anarchism*, London: 1963.

ARTICLES

Abbot, W. C. "English Conspiracies and Dissent", *American Historical Review*, 13, April, July, 1907.

Blanchard, Paul. "The Man Who Killed Verwoerd", *Encounter*, 28, March, 1967.

Buckley, W. F. "Politics of Assassination", *Esquire*, 70, Oct., 1968.

DeWar, Hugo. "Murder Revisited: The Case of Sergei Mironovich Kirov", *Problems of Communism*, 14, Sept.-Oct., 1965.

Dietze, Gottfried. "Will the Presidency Incite Assassination?", *Ethics*, 77, Oct., 1965.

Hardman, J. "Terrorism", *Encyclopedia of the Social Sciences*, New York: 1933.

Hilliard, J. L. "Counter-Subversive Operations in Urban Areas", *Military Review*, 46, June, 1966.

Howe, Irving. "Political Terrorism: Hysteria on the Left", *New York Times Magazine*, April 12, 1970.

Janis, Irving. "Effects of Fear Arousal on Attitude Change",

Berkowitz, L. ed. *Advances in Social Psychology*, III, New York: 1961.

Kelly, Joseph B. "Assassination in War-Time", *Military Law Review*, 30, Oct., 1965.

Lerner, Max. "Assassination", *Encyclopedia of the Social Sciences*, New York: 1933.

Margihella, Carlos. "Mini-Manual of the Urban Guerrilla", 6, *Tri-Continental*, June, 1969.

Mazrui, Ali A. "Thoughts on Assassination in Africa", *Political Science Quarterly*, 83, March, 1968.

Moss, Robert. "Urban Guerrillas in Latin America", *Conflict Studies*, 8, Oct., 1970.

Moss, Robert. "Uruguay: Terrorism versus Democracy", *Conflict Studies*, 14, Aug., 1971.

Padover, Saul K. "Patterns of Assassination in Occupied Territory", *Public Opinion Quarterly*, 7, Winter, 1943.

Rapoport, David C. "Coup d'Etat: The Views of the Men Firing Pistols", C. J. Friedrich, ed. *Revolution*, New York: 1968.

Rapoport, David C. "The Political Dimensions of Military Usurpation", *Political Science Quarterly*, 83, Dec., 1968.

Remak, J. "Sarajevo—Design and Accident", *Journal of Central European Affairs*, 21, July, Oct., 1961.

Roucek, Joseph S. "Sociological Elements of a Theory of Terror and Violence", *American Journal of Economics and Sociology*, 21, Spring, 1962.

Silverman, Jerry and P. Jackson. "Terror in Insurgency Warfare", *Military Review*, 50, Oct., 1970.

Thornton, Thomas P. "Terror as a Weapon of Political Agitation", H. Eckstein, ed. *Internal War*, New York: 1964.

Tishendorf, Alfred. "The Assassination of Chief Executives in Latin America", *South Atlantic Quarterly*, 60, Winter, 1961

Withey, Stephen B. "Reaction to Uncertain Threats", Baker, G. W. and D. W. Chapman, eds. *Man and Society in Disaster*, New York: 1962.